AWAKENING TO PRAYER

Awakening to Prayer

A

WOMAN'S

PERSPECTIVE

Clare Wagner

ST. ANTHONY MESSENGER PRESS
Cincinnati, Ohio

. . . .

Dedicated to the memory of Diane Langeteig,
witness to transforming grace,
and Baby Clarence Patrick Wagner,
witness to the treasure each life is.

. . . .

Excerpts from "Du, Nachbar, Gott.../You, God, who live next door...", from *Rilke's Book of Hours: Love Poems to God* by Rainer Maria Rilke, translated by Anita Barrows and Joanna Macy, copyright © 1996 by Anita Barrows and Joanna Macy. Used by permission of Riverhead Books, an imprint of Penguin Group (USA) Inc.; "Mystery" from *Missa Gaia*. Written by Jeremy Geffen. Published by Kabir Music (ASCAP). Administered in the United States and Canada by Living Earth Music c/o Helene Blue Musique Ltd.; from *Hope Through Heartstrings* by Mattie J.T. Stepanek. Copyright © 2002 Mattie J.T. Stepanek. Reprinted by Permission of Hyperion. All rights reserved; from "The Big Heart" and "The Rowing Endeth" from *The Awful Rowing Toward God* by Anne Sexton. Copyright © 1975 by Loring Conant, Jr., executor of the estate of Anne Sexton. Reprinted by permission of Houghton Mifflin Harcourt Publishing Company. All rights reserved; from poem by Dawna Markova is from *Women Pray: Voices through the Ages, from Many Faiths, Cultures and Traditions* © 2001 by Monica Furlong (Woodstock, VT: SkyLight Paths Publishing). Permission granted by SkyLight Paths Publishing, P.O. Box 237, Woodstock, VT 05091 www.skylightpaths.com.; from the Penguin publication *The Gift, Poems by Hafiz*, copyright 1999 Daniel Ladinsky and used with his permission.

Scripture passages have been taken from *New Revised Standard Version Bible*, copyright ©1989 by the Division of Christian Education of the National Council of the Churches of Christ in the U.S.A., and used by permission. All rights reserved.

Cover and book design by Mark Sullivan.
Cover image © istockphoto.com/Soubrette

LIBRARY OF CONGRESS CATALOGING-IN-PUBLICATION DATA
Wagner, Clare.
Awakening to prayer : a woman's perspective / Clare Wagner.
p. cm.
Includes bibliographical references (p.   ) and index.
ISBN 978-0-86716-892-1 (pbk. : alk. paper) 1. Catholic women—Religious life. 2. Prayer—Catholic Church. I. Title.
BX2353.W34 2009
248.3'2082—dc22
　　　　　　　　　　　2008048383

ISBN: 978-0-86716-892-1

Copyright ©2009, Clare Wagner. All rights reserved.

Published by St. Anthony Messenger Press
28 W. Liberty St.
Cincinnati, OH 45202
www.SAMPBooks.org

Printed in the United States of America.

Printed on acid-free paper.

09 10 11 12 13   5 4 3 2 1

I wish to acknowledge the support and encouragement of an organization of philanthropists: Foundations and Donors Interested in Catholic Activities (FADICA). In January of 2005, I was invited to speak before this organization at a conference entitled Women of Faith. The discussion explored the many contributions of women to Roman Catholic ministry, church leadership and theology.

The members of FADICA heard my appeal for a renewed focus on women's spirituality in the context of significant religious change during the twentieth century and the pressing challenges of the twenty-first. The need for a creative, solidly grounded, and theologically sophisticated spirituality available in an accessible form for all Christian women seemed obvious. Follow-up conversations by the FADICA board, ably led by Frank Butler, led to a proposal from Fairfield University for a series of books on women's spirituality. Thus, FADICA, Fairfield University, and St. Anthony Messenger Press formed a collaborative partnership to produce seven volumes under the title *Called to Holiness: Spirituality for Catholic Women.*

I wish to thank individuals and foundations whose generosity made this collaborative venture possible. These include the Amaturo Family Foundation, the AMS Fund, the Cushman Foundation, the Mary J. Donnelly Foundation, George and Marie Doty, Mrs. James Farley, the Robert and Maura Burke Morey Charitable Trust, Maureen O'Leary, Ann Marie Paine and the Raskob Foundation for Catholic Activities. I wish to extend a word of thanks and praise to the entire FADICA membership, whose conscientious, quiet and loving participation in shaping the life of the church has been an inspiration.

*The focus of this series is spirituality. Its interest is women of all back-*grounds: rich and poor; married and single; white, black and brown; gay and straight; those who are biological mothers and those who are mothers in other senses. There will be volumes on grassroots theology, family life, prayer, action for justice, grieving, young adult life, the wisdom years and Hispanic heritage. I hope all the volumes in this series will deepen and shape your own spiritual life in creative ways, as you engage with the theology of our rich, two-thousand-year-old Christian tradition.

Women's spiritualities are lived in light of their concrete, specific experiences of joy and struggle; ecstasy and despair; virtue and vice; work and leisure; family and friends; embodiment and sexuality; tears and laughter; sickness and health; sistering and mothering. These volumes are for women and men from all walks of life, whether they are new to the spiritual journey or old hands, affluent, middle-class or poor. Included in the circle we call church are persons from every country on the planet, some at the center, others at the margins or even beyond.

The time is ripe for "ordinary" women to be doing theology. The first and second waves of the women's movement in the nineteenth and twentieth centuries provided a valiant and solid foundation for the third wave which will mark, and be marked by, the world of the early twenty-first century. Changes and developments from one generation to the next make our heads spin. Younger women readers are likely to be already grooming the soil for a fourth wave of Christian spirituality done by and for women. Women have always loved God, served others and struggled with sin, but the historical context has been less than friendly in terms of women's dignity, acknowledgment of female gifts and empowerment by church and society. In a time of growing emphasis on the role of clergy, and the backlash against women in society, the voices of the laity—especially the voices of women—are needed more than ever.

The Greek language has two words for time. *Chronos* points to the time signaled by the hands on the clock—for example, it is a quarter past two. *Kairos* points to time that is ripe, a moment pregnant with possibility. As Christian women, we live in a time rightly described as *kairos*. It is a time that calls us, demands of us renewed energy, reflection and commitment to attend to and help each other grow spiritually as we seek to love ourselves and the world. At this point in history, the fruit of women's struggle includes new self-awareness, self-confidence and self-respect. More and more women are beginning to see just how lovable and capable they are. The goal of the Christian life has always been to lay down our lives in love for the other, but the particular ways this vocation is lived out differ from era to era and place to place. Women's ability to voice with confidence the phrase, "I am a theologian" at the beginning of the twenty-first century means something it could not have meant even fifty years ago.

Those who were part of the early waves of feminism celebrate the hard-won accomplishments of the women's movement and know that this work needs to be taken up by future generations. Young women in their twenties and thirties are often unaware of past efforts that brought about more dignity and freedom for women. Women have opened many doors, but many remain closed. The media have recently explored the plight of Hindu widows in India; less publicized is that women in the United States still earn only seventy-seven cents for every dollar earned by their male counterparts. We must be vigilant and continue to act for decades to come in order to secure our accomplishments thus far and make further inroads toward the creation of a just, egalitarian world. Those who sense that the women's movement is in a doldrums inspire us to renew the enthusiasm and dedication of our foremothers.

When we cast our eye beyond the women of our own nation, it takes but a split-second to realize that the majority of the world's poor and oppressed are women. A quick visit to the Women's Rights section of the Human Rights Watch Web site reveals the breadth and depth of women's oppression across the globe from poverty and domestic abuse to sex slavery. Most women (and their children) do not have enough to eat, a warm, dry place to sleep or access to education. Female babies are more at risk than male babies. Women, more than men, lack the protection of the law and the respect of their communities. The double-standard in sexual matters affects women in harmful ways in all cultures and economic groups across the globe.

For all of these reasons it is not just important—but pressing, crucial, urgent—that all women of faith own the title "theologian" and shape this role in light of each woman's unique set of characteristics, context, relationships and spiritualities. We are theologians when we sort through our experience and the great and small problems of our time through reflection on Scripture or the words of a mystic or theologian. The images of God that emerged for Paul, Augustine or Catherine of Siena provide guidance, but their theology cannot ever be a substitute for our own. Theology helps us shape what we think about God, justice, love, the destiny of humanity and the entire universe in a way that is relevant to the specific issues facing us in the twenty-first century. The call to spiritual depths and mystical heights has never been more resounding.

Elizabeth A. Dreyer
Series Editor

Awakening to prayer is becoming increasingly conscious of the most holy Mystery to whom we are invited, encouraged to relate. The word *prayer* is almost as generic as *food* or *book*. And the varieties of prayer forms are countless. Images of prayer that come to mind are of a mother kneeling at her child's bedside at night, a community saying the prayer Jesus taught with hands and hearts joined, a solitary figure standing, head bowed, in a cemetery, or hundreds of people in a mosque bowing down in reverent homage. In this best and worst of times, it is intriguing to ponder how women of the twenty-first century enter into a relationship with Holy Presence. It has been a challenge not to repeat what has already been well said about prayer. I have found it enlivening and engaging to realize that at this moment of enormous change, rapid technological advancement and a new relationship between faith and science, we are called upon to see prayer, too, in new, creative ways.

When we are most conscious of the beauty of creation, the wonders of technology and how well everything is going, what is there to say to God? When we are keenly aware of the tragedy of war, the unfairness of poverty or some very difficult personal struggle, where is God anyway?

God is everywhere. The ramifications of that simple statement are what this book is about. Whether you are nurturing, struggling, thirsting—whatever dimensions of daily or global life are front and center for you, Holy Presence permeates every "cell" of your experience. Awakening to prayer is noticing the intimacy between all aspects of your life and God.

In this book, I draw on the wisdom of the Scriptures, the insights of the mystics and the experience of ordinary, vibrant women and men living in our midst. Though I offer suggestions of words to use and rituals to experience, new words aren't the important part. Rather, awakening to prayer is coming to see that separation from Divine Mystery is an illusion. Spirituality is a journey that lasts a lifetime. That journey itself is home, and prayer is its foundation as you travel.

CHAPTER ONE

• Noticing •

I think that every discovery of the world plunges us into jubilation,
a radical amazement that tears apart the veil of triviality.[1]
—Dorothee Soelle

Prayer is large and deep, a reality we have considered essential in our faith,
yet understood in a wide variety of ways. Its definition is illusive. Its
experience is undeniable. Its goal is communion with the Divine. For
those who desire to enter this mystery of prayer and relationship with
the Divine, noticing is essential. There is, of course, ordinary noticing
and deep noticing. Though *every* discovery of the world may not plunge
us into jubilation, deep noticing does "tear apart the veil of triviality"
and put us face-to-face with what is real and amazing. In the realm of
ordinary noticing, as you reflect on this day in your life, you may have
noticed whether it was cloudy or sunny when you got up, whether it
was noisy or quiet and what you had for breakfast. Also, you may have
noticed the sound of an infant turning in her bed, that the dogs need
to go out or the mood of your partner. On this ordinary day, if you
noticed very little, that's all right; this isn't a test. See what tomorrow
brings. While the culture in which we live demands a great deal of
looking and watching, noticing is not a value that is promoted. And if
we move almost always in the fast lane, a lot is missed. Shortly after
9/11, leaders suggested that people go right on with life—keep buying,

traveling and entertaining in a "normal" way. There was strong encouragement not to notice that because of this attack the world would never be the same. Such an event is something quite major not to notice.

Later chapters will address noticing the larger world in which we live. In this chapter, the focus is a personal kind of noticing which in itself can be prayer. In contrast to watching, noticing involves entering in, going beneath the surface. This kind of noticing is the difference between looking at a person's eyes and noting that the eyes are brown, a bit bloodshot, deep set or not, and looking into someone's eyes and seeing sadness or joy, actually seeing that person's soul. This kind of seeing comes to mind in the image and experience of a new mother beholding her infant. Perhaps the word *beholding* is a key in the connection between noticing and prayer. In the past year, I had an experience of "beholding" my grandnephew. Brennan was a month old and had experienced trauma right after birth. He had a heart problem and was whisked away from his parents to a children's hospital. At the time of my visit he was doing well and I was allowed to hold him. Brennan gave me the gift of an extended time of eye contact in which neither of us so much as blinked. I saw the beauty in his fragile little body and the magnificence of his courageous little soul. I noticed a movement within me which I now name an exchange of love and deep respect; it was communion. In this experience was prayer—the "in-breaking" of God—facilitated by the gaze of an infant and an older woman noticing his graced body/spirit. Welling up in me was gratitude.

Joan Chittister writes that, "the purpose of prayer is to prepare our own hearts for the in-breaking of God...for the burst of awareness, when it comes, that God is not somewhere else, God is here, now, in our own hearts."[2] Every day doesn't bring an experience like the encounter I just described. However, each day offers possibilities and the opportunity to be aware of what is going on within and outside of us. This attitude of noticing and paying attention creates a context for awareness of Sacred Presence, of living always on the edge of mystery.

Perhaps this is what Saint Paul had in mind when he entreated the early Christians to pray without ceasing (see 1 Thessalonians 5:17).

A simple yet profound definition of contemplation is "a long, loving look at the real."[3] An important place to engage this practice is within ourselves, our own bodies, minds, hearts. To contemplate our inner terrain with that "long, loving look" invites a pilgrimage. Though all of us are aware of our bodies, minds and spirits in many ways, and we remember experiences that move us, to take a look, "a long, loving look" may be an infrequent event. At this very moment as you read, pause to notice your body, your mind, your heart.

Attentiveness to Our Sacred Vessels—Our Bodies

Women's bodies are wonderfully made and hold intimate knowledge of the process of creating life. Our bodies—young, middle-aged or old—demand our attention. It's hard to ignore hormonal activity, birthing, tension, wounding, bursts of energy and the countless inner events of a woman's body. In a sense, the interiority needed for contemplation is second nature to women. Our bodies offer us a deeper sense of inner workings than is common for males. However, history and culture as far back as the story of Eve, and even earlier, have not encouraged women to see their bodies as subjects worthy of contemplation. More than twenty years ago, in pointing out how women were perceived, Rosemary Reuther wrote, "As a symbol of the body, sexuality and maternity, woman represents the evil lower nature."[4] Sadly, that perception is so ingrained in the culture that the world is still in recovery from that terrible misconception. We have been affected by a long history of seeing woman's body as object, servant, workhorse and never "good" enough. The fact that we haven't recovered from the misconception is evident in the escalation of elective surgeries for body improvement and the increases in bulimia and anorexia that plead for the healing of this societal wound.

Just to notice our bodies, to look lovingly, to touch with tenderness this face, arm, heart of ours, begins healing, not only for ourselves but for all the world's women as well. We are linked to the pull of the moon and the tides of the ocean through our menstrual cycle; we are made of elements with which the stars gifted us; the capacity to breathe life in and out is amazing. We are God's work of art; we are "temples" of the very Spirit of God. The universe needs us to notice these things.

Making a choice for a pilgrimage into ourselves brings with it a need to be humble and open, not controlling what we find or judging it—simply noticing what is there. Few of us may find what artist Meinrad Craighead saw in an interior noticing of hers, and yet it is worth taking note of the marvels we may discover in inner space. Meinrad writes, "What my eyes saw meshed with images I carried inside my body. Pictures printed on the walls of my womb began to emerge,"[5] and from those pictures came her series of unique images collected in her book, *The Mother's Songs*. A woman's body holds in its cells all that life has presented to her—the tenderness, the glory moments, the wounds of her own and of her ancestors, the momentous joys and also great personal and universal sadnesses. This pilgrimage of body noticing is sacred; the body is honored simply by not being ignored or disdained. Ann Hillman writes that, "Becoming tender, becoming flesh—the real, vulnerable human beings that we are—creates an honest container for the rest of the journey."[6] This noble "container" merits exploration and appreciation.

Christian theology affected by hierarchical dualism has historically separated matter and spirit. It has equated spirit with the masculine principle and matter with the feminine principle. It places women and the earth lower than men and spirit. Letting go of this dualistic perspective is a major work of contemporary theology, particularly feminist theology. Once one embraces a perspective free of hierarchical dualism, it is possible to notice that the "container," the flesh, a woman's body is the dwelling place of the very Spirit of God. And the earth, too, is sacred. This is important information for a pilgrimage of body awareness.

A Matter of the Heart

Of course, body, mind and heart are dimensions of a whole person, but bear with separating them for the sake of a way to make an inner pilgrimage. What in our hearts should we notice for the sake of relating more fully to our God, ourselves, our world? In ancient biblical traditions, the heart is seen as the locus of emotional activity: spiritual experiences of grief, sadness, joy and deep peace. It is seen as the center of wisdom and decision-making. To "set the heart" is to give careful attention to what is immediate with determination and intent. The heart is the place of our plans and purposes, the source of our thoughts and deeds. The heart symbolizes a person's deep center, the place where desire for love lives and from which love emanates. Our physical hearts beat and pause rhythmically and continuously; if they do not, we are not alive. The significance of the heart as a physical organ and the symbol of the heart as the spiritual center open an arena of awareness that draws us to the sacred, that has the power to move us to a place of awe.

In determining how we are going to move into the activity of noticing all that is in our hearts, I find it helpful to turn to poets who have found words to describe the pilgrimage. As Meinrad Craighead saw images in her womb that fed her heart and moved her to create paintings, the poet Anne Sexton noticed amazing things in her heart when she took that "long, loving look." This verse describes some of what she discovered. The poet speaks of her heart as large as a watermelon and wise and full. She goes on to describe that fullness.

Big heart,
wide as a watermelon
but wise as birth,
there is so much abundance
in the people I have:
Max, Lois, Joe, Louise,
Joan, Marie, Dawn,
Arlene, Father Dunne,

and all in their short lives
give to me repeatedly,
in the way the sea
places its many fingers on the shore,
again and again
and they know me,
they help me unravel,
they listen with ears made of
conch shells. . .
They are my staff.
They comfort me.[7]

This poet had a heart of flesh, not of stone. She was "big-hearted" in her willingness to let people into her heart, to "unravel" with them. She noticed what they did within and who they were in relation to herself. Anne Sexton was aware of wisdom in her heart and abundant life in the relationships of her heart. She saw that life manifested itself in the way her companions held her as gently as the shore holds the sea, listening and responding with the best wine, one might say, the cup of blessing. She implies that these people are Divine Presence to her—"they are my staff, they comfort me" (see Psalm 23).

Accepting the invitation to make a pilgrimage into your heart is in itself a contemplative act. It is neither complicated nor esoteric to pray in this manner. It is an effort to be authentic about who you are and discover the abundance and deficiencies you find within. This isn't navel-gazing; this practice opens the seeker's eyes to what is real within her. Each person carries a world in her heart, a world worthy of notice, of exploration. This journey is also a crucial part of our spiritual journey and prayer. It is hard to overestimate the significance for a spiritual journey of noticing who and what we carry in our hearts. Wisdom itself is seated and grows in the mind-heart connection. To separate mind from heart, to glorify rationality, is a source of danger in contemporary society.

In a book entitled *The Crone*, I read a story long ago which stays in my memory. It's about observation and about wisdom. In primitive societies, long before we had sophisticated knowledge of how the human body functioned, people simply observed and came to conclusions by trusting what they noticed over time. These peoples had enormous respect for life and for women as source of life and blood as symbol of life. They observed that women ceased having their periods when they were pregnant. They concluded that the blood that was ordinarily released was being used to nurture the child within its mother's womb. Later, when women reached what we call menopause, again the monthly blood flow ceased. Because they believed in the principle of eternal becoming, and noticed growth and depth in older women, they concluded that the blood, or life source, that was not being released was being used to birth and nurture wisdom within the woman, the wise crone.[8] Rooted in experience, based on careful noticing, the conclusions reached hold truths that served the people well and affected their worship and behavior, especially the way they regarded women.

An Open Mind

This story of ancient observation is a reminder of beholding reality and allowing it to reveal deep truth. It is a good example of body-heart/spirit-mind functioning in harmony and leading to profound revelation. Continuing the inward pilgrimage toward consideration of the mind is a challenge in a different way than the noticing of body and heart. It is different in that we have a strong sense that we can more fully control what our minds do. Often, women of faith resist consideration of questions, doubts or criticisms that arise from reading, praying, experiencing life. This is not helpful. Our desires for a conscious, deep connection with God are thwarted by deliberately not noticing or refusing to work with something that comes to consciousness. The call to prayer, the way of authentically walking a spiritual path, is to be open to the real and allow that reality to lead us, perhaps not pain-free, to God.

It is common that women enter into a spiritual guidance relationship when they notice doubts about church, about doctrines, about
prayer itself. Often personal or global experiences raise doubts or serious questions. These situations are not uncommon:

- I have a gay son. How does my church welcome him?
- If God is all-powerful, how is it that God does not cure my
  child of leukemia?
- Why is it that Jesus included everyone at his table, but my
  friend is not welcome at Eucharist?

These are questions to live with, speak about with others, ponder in
contemplative silence—even welcome as an invitation to go deeper into
your faith. To continually evolve spiritually means to go beyond our
self-protected shell, to leave behind the certainty of unexamined faith
and prayer life. Our minds have a tremendous role in letting the scales
fall from our eyes and seeing anew. Things we read, thoughts we ponder, dialogues we enter, and just plain critical thinking have a great role
in moving us to the margins of "conventional wisdom" and leading us
to the center of deep reality. And, of course, minds can be tricksters, too.

Faith stories from ancient times, scriptural times and from just yes-
terday can nurture twenty-first century women on a spiritual path.
What is important is that we approach those stories or myths with
"attentive engagement, cultivated awareness and a taste for wisdom."[9]
Noticing what is present and emerging in our bodies, hearts and minds,
developing a habit of awareness within us and around us, and searching
for the way of wisdom through contemplation, prepares us for the in-
breaking of God in any moment.

This long, loving look at the real, to which this chapter invites you,
opens but one possible way to pray. It is the eyes-open way of noticing
the world of your own body, heart and mind. The beauty of this kind of
journey is captured by Elizabeth Johnson: "Contemplation is a way of
seeing that leads to communion. The fact that the world (of the body,

mind, heart) is simply there, in splendor and fragility, giv·
der, leading to a religious sense of the loving power that quickens .

FOOD FOR THOUGHT

1. As you consider women's bodies, especially attitudes of past theology
and of culture toward them, what negative notions do you absorb? As
you contemplate your body today, notice and name the sacred aspects
of it—the work of your hands, the words you speak and so on.
2. Hold your hand over your heart. Listen to its continuous life-giving
beat, notice the people you carry in your heart and name them, those
you love. Can you recall a recent "experience of the heart" with one
of these persons? Reimagine the incident and the feelings you knew
then. If you feel drawn to do so, breathe deeply and slowly, repeating
as you inhale this name for God: Source of Love, Source of Love...
3. Drawing on the knowledge of your mind, heart and body, name what
it is that you know with great conviction about your relationship with
God and faith as well as your doubts and questions. Jot down your
response in a journal if that is helpful.

RITUAL

1. Light a candle. Place a cloth and a picture of yourself on a table. Take
time to breathe deeply for a bit; place your hands first on your solar
plexus, which is that area of your body just above your abdomen, next
on your heart and then on your forehead honoring body, heart and
mind.
2. Pray this prayer: Praise to you, Sacred Loving Presence. You long to
gift us with your love; we long to open our bodies, minds and hearts
to awareness of your presence within us and everywhere. Help us to
know that we are wondrously made. Open our eyes to incredible possibilities present in our everyday lives. Amen.
3. Make a bow that brings your head below your heart to honor wisdom, oneness and humility.

CHAPTER TWO

• Awakening •

The desiring heart expands with boundless compassion in myriad communities around the globe, and the dawn of a transformed world is on the horizon.[1]

—Mary Grey

It's very early in the morning, the alarm goes off, a baby cries, your wakeup call from the motel clerk comes; it's time to get up. Like it or not, your sleeping time is over, at least for now. Would you like to sleep longer? That is understandable. Are there things in your personal life or your awareness of the world that make pulling the covers over your head a very strong temptation? That, too, is understandable.

Pulling the covers over your head and wanting to go back to sleep is understandable whether we are talking about sleep as a physical reality or as a symbol of wanting to escape or hide from difficult things in our world. At times, the world becomes too much to bear, with its wars, poverty and sadness. When you perceive that indeed "the world is too much with us"—then sleep or turning away may be exactly the appropriate state in which to nurture your body, mind and spirit. However, having acknowledged the need to turn away from the world's concerns at this time, the spiritually alive woman can still choose, with the help of prayer and friends and faith, to be wide awake to the world as it is.

In the first chapter, we focused on noticing the world within—the body, the heart, the mind. In this chapter on awakening, we pay attention to the external world which continuously affects us. The beauty of creation can serve as a major source of awakening and also a fine reason to stay awake. The universe, including scientists' constant new discoveries, is a source of wonder, amazement and creativity. Its incredible evolutionary activity not only keeps us awake, it can move us to awe and to songs of praise and gratitude. Because of the universe's continual dance of birthing and destruction, of great beauty and of disturbing chaos, we are sometimes awakened by an earthquake rather than a sunrise.

Instruments of Awakening: Sunrises and Earthquakes
Our lives are each so unique in terms of what awakens our spirit, calls us to new awareness, forcefully invites us to notice the presence of God. For some of us, it may be literally the beauty of a sunrise. It's also possible to see other life experiences as sunrises—for example, someone saying, "I love you," or the birth of a baby, or the completion of your dissertation, or holding a first grandchild. These "sunrises" awaken us, move us to gratitude and joy and help us sense the in-breaking of God in our lives. Sometimes we express that feeling in words that are prayer. On the other hand, there are the "earthquake" times—the loss of a loved one, a cancer diagnosis, a war that evokes despair in us, a fire, a flood, a Darfur. These things shock us awake, and it takes time to respond. When that happens, we cry out for help and for mercy. We look to family and friends and God for compassionate presence. That is our prayer. It's possible to miss beauty and ugliness, creativity and destruction with one's head and heart, literally or figuratively under the covers or asleep. Awakening is intimately related to our life journey in the Spirit and to the prayer and the action which flows from it.

If I stay under the covers, stay asleep to what is real, rather than letting it in or taking a long, loving look at it, what will call me to prayer? What will move me to reach out to my neighbor? In the town where I live there is a "Race for the Cure" for cancer every June. For a number

12

of years I thought about running; then two dear friends were diagnosed with cancer. I became very involved in their struggle and moved by their courage. Nothing could keep me from that run. An "earthquake" pulled the covers from my head, moved me to closer relationship, prayer and action. Both gratitude and crying out for help permeated my prayer, and the experience enriched my life.

Through God's initiative, the invitation to relationship with the sacred is living within us. That invitation is further clarified and opened up through the universe and its evolving life, through Jesus' consciousness and experience of God's love. If, as Ruth Burrows states, prayer is essentially what God does and that "what God is doing for us is giving us the divine Self in love,"[2] what is our part? As with all significant invitations from those important or close to us, we need to respond. This need and desire to respond points to the intimate connection between awakening and prayer. How do we become conscious of the invitation to relationship with Mystery, with the Life of all life? How can deep stirrings within us evoked by "sunrises" or "earthquakes" be turned into words or silences of prayer?

Jesus, Consistently Wide Awake

Scripture teaches us how to wake up and gives us hints of the path to greater consciousness and to relationship with God. For example, the disciples who were put to sleep by fear and grief were gathered in the Upper Room when suddenly wind, fire and Spirit catapulted them into awareness. Words were given, and we can be quite sure that they awakened fully (see Acts 2:1–13). Another story that exemplifies a different way of coming to see anew is the story of the blind man in Mark's Gospel. After Jesus touched his eyes, he saw people, but they looked like trees walking around. Jesus touched his eyes a second time and he "saw everything clearly" (Mark 8:25). The first awakening was sudden and dramatic; however, this story reminds us that awakening is a process. Only gradually do things get clear about prayer, about life, about how to see a given situation.

The Gospel stories give evidence of Jesus as a wide awake human being who knew himself to be in the grip of the power of God's unconditional love. He was awake to these realities:

- The exclusion of the Samaritan woman at the well (see John 4:7–42).
- The need of the woman who touched his garment for healing (see Luke 8:43–48).
- The courage of the woman who anointed his feet (see Mark 14:3–9).
- The suffering of the woman found in adultery (see John 8:3–11).
- The appropriateness of healing on the Sabbath (see Mark 3:1–6).
- The imaginative power in himself to birth the Prodigal Son story (see Luke 15:11–32).

We see in these events Jesus' consciousness of himself and his world which shaped his behavior, moved him to prayerful expression and enabled him to take the risks demanded by integrity.

As your sacred life has unfolded thus far, what experiences of awakening have been yours? Have you fallen in love, given birth, lived near the ocean, watched a garden grow, faced a life-threatening disease or lost a dear friend or family member? Any of those things and many other experiences, small and momentous, may have awakened you to deep stirrings within you. To choose to stay awake to those stirrings can lead you to the silence and the words that serve as entry into the Mystery, into relationship with the Spirit dwelling within you.

One of my most memorable calls to consciousness was the first time I witnessed the birth of a baby. The mother was a seventeen-year-old girl who was not married, and I was there because no one else could be. These challenging circumstances did not interfere with my being able to receive the gift of the miracle of new life. I shall be forever grateful to that dear and courageous seventeen-year-old. Much to my surprise, the ramifications of that experience were far-reaching. Several years later, in a theology class, I was asked to write a paper tracing my resistance to nuclear proliferation and war. As I began to reflect and prepare, what arose with great force in me was the memory of that little girl's birth. And it made great sense—the beauty, cost, fragility of a life realized in seeing that birth stirred deep within me a commitment to resist whatever threatens or devalues a life. Sometimes we know only much later how one powerful experience affects the choices, behaviors and convictions that become integral to our spiritual stance. And it is out of that stance, faithful to those deep stirrings, that we make our way into the Mystery with growing consciousness.

A Poet, a Journalist and Their Wide-Awake Spirits

Thus, a key component of spiritual awakening is paying attention to the significance, even the potential significance, of life experiences. Two very different contemporary authors whose awakened hearts have given the world "sacred texts" of a new era come to mind. Mattie Stepanek wrote books of poetry that were on the *New York Times* bestseller list. Mattie was born with a serious illness that took his life at age thirteen. Some deep stirrings in Mattie, to which he paid attention, made him aware of his call to be a poet and a peacemaker. He began writing poetry at age three and dreamed of meeting Jimmy Carter, whom he admired for his peacemaking efforts. His call was every bit as powerful as that of Samuel in the Bible or of any disciple. In his short life, he opened himself to the Spirit and opened the hearts of his readers to a path toward peace. The following excerpt is from a poem Mattie wrote shortly after September 11, 2001:

> We need to stop.
> Just stop.
> Stop for a moment...
> Before anybody

Says or does anything
That may hurt anyone else.
We need to be silent.
Just silent.
Silent for a moment...
Before we forever lose
The blessing of songs
That grow in our hearts.
We need to notice.
Just notice.
Notice for a moment...
Before the future slips away
Into ashes and dust of humility.[3]

Since this young boy was so wide awake, so conscious at an early age, he reflects in his poem a Spirit-filled way to respond to deep experience whether it is tragic or beautiful. To stop, to be silent and to notice, suggests a process in which we allow an experience, ordinary or extraordinary, to pierce through our defenses. Awakening can happen this way.

Another awakened author whom I find inspiring is National Public Radio reporter Anne Garrels. Her book *Naked in Baghdad* is an account of her experience in Iraq during the United States invasion. In addition to her honest reporting of heartbreaking events, the book contains e-mails from her husband who reports Anne's experiences to family and friends. Of course, I know very little of Anne's spiritual life other than what her book reveals. But somewhere in her depths, she heard a call and was graced with the courage to report on some of the most dangerous world events in current history. Among those are the fall of the Soviet Union, the United States' involvement in Kosovo and the Iraq war. In *Naked in Baghdad*, she writes, "I feel as if I am in a cocoon, documenting the small world that I can see."[4] Anne's mission is truthtelling and, in faithfulness to that mission, she invites us to be as awake as she is to the lives caught in conflict, the untold grieving and the insurmountable cost of war, to attend to those whose skills, unerring honesty and compassion have the power to open "the small world that I can see" to all of us. This story of a defining moment of our time told with Anne Garrels's accuracy and clarity holds the power to awaken, to inform and to bring us to our knees.

The Mystical in All of Us

Your life, as well as the lives of Mattie and Anne, testify to the presence of Spirit in us and in the universe. Belief in this underlying power of the divine makes it possible to awaken and respond to whatever is, no matter how challenging. Long ago and in different difficult times, women and men were graced to see not only what was in their world, but also the Spirit present in all of it. Hildegard of Bingen, a twelfth-century mystic, wrote about Spirit in a way that is extravagant and assuring. This Spirit permeates creation, continuously offering life and hope—no matter what:

> I, the highest and fiery power, have kindled every living spark and I have breathed out nothing that can die.... I flame above the beauty of the fields; I shine in the waters; in the sun, the moon and the stars, I burn. And by means of the airy wind, I stir everything into quickness with a certain invisible life which sustains all... I, the fiery power, lie hidden in these things and they blaze from me.[5]

Throughout the history of religious traditions, the people called mystics have left us with writings about God, prayer and the spiritual life which, for many centuries, were seldom mentioned in homilies or adult faith-formation classes. That is changing, and our eyes are being opened to prayer experiences that have been hidden for too long. Rather than dismissing the mystics as people from another planet or odd religious fanatics, it is possible to be inspired and encouraged by the experiences of the divine they offer us. Why not ponder the mystery of Spirit as "fiery power" that shines in water, sun, moon and stars, as "stirring everything into quickness?"

Why not awaken to the possibility that we can all be mystics? Dorothee Soelle writes of "democratizing" the concept of mysticism, of looking at everyday experiences with mystical sensibilities. She suggests that we begin this awakening by noticing what happens in love, "when people give themselves wholly and without reserve to another human being." Such experiences deserve to be called mystical. In an experience of true and wholehearted love, features of mystical experience are present: a sense of oneness with all, a letting go of ego, discovery of the deep and real self, amazement and great joy.[6] Recall, if you can, experiences in which all or some of those characteristics were present. Are your own mystical sensibilities dormant within you, waiting to be awakened? Or are they flowering, giving cause for joy and thanksgiving?

Mystical experience, simply stated, is knowing God experientially—not only because of what a book, a friend or an authority said, but rather because of what happened in your own mind, heart and soul. There is a "place" in us where the human and the divine touch. From that place experience of the sacred springs forth. No one told Hildegard that the Spirit shone in the sun, moon and stars. No one told Meister Eckehart that what God did all day was lie on a maternity bed continually giving birth. No one told Teresa of Avila that within us is a rich palace built of gold and precious stones and that we were not hollow inside. No one told Mechtilde of Magdeburg that the day of her spiritual awakening was the day she saw all things in God and God in all things.

These people of prayer who went before us show us the way to trust our experience, to see it as sacred, to awaken to the possibilities of relationship with Divine Spirit. They provide us with hints of how we might walk the path of spiritual awareness and prayer in the twenty-first century. Our images may differ from those of past centuries due to our cultural milieu. Music, technology and new scientific information offer us language unknown in previous centuries or even previous decades. We need these new images. After pondering an experience of your own and recognizing its spiritual dimensions, you can describe it in your own words. The Spirit is present today in our ordinary and unusual experiences of life; our call is to be open and to be awake.

The Heartbeat of God in All Experience

Being open to the Divine in our midst births hope and courage. This experience is not just for our sakes but it is also for God's sake and the sake of the universe. This moment in history is filled with both creativity and destruction—perhaps all moments are. However, there also appears to be a remarkable and growing spiritual awareness in the human community. God makes the *New York Times* bestseller list, talk shows and newspapers regularly. Though the Holy One might not smile on all of it, there certainly is evidence of a search. There are more and more centering prayer groups and meditation centers across the country and numerous people seek spiritual guides and authentic prayer experiences. It is amazing and cause for celebration.

On the other hand, I recently heard a speaker characterize our time as the dark night of our species. She was awake to violence among nations and in city streets, corruption in business and government and the continued victimization of the poor and oppressed. The heavy hand of patriarchal domination is exerting its power in churches and many other systems of the world. As I mentioned early in this chapter, there is much in our global and, perhaps, personal world that makes us want to stay asleep. Sometimes it's a great idea to turn off the news, to take a day to escape from all that burdens the human heart; in fact, that is a wise woman's activity. Yet, those deep inner stirrings and the call of the Divine, of God, is to be awake to what is. Awakening prayer moves us into the energy of the sacred which enhances and protects our souls. Prayer is a conduit of healing grace in the world. In the dark nights that are personal, species-wide or affecting the whole of creation, the heartbeat of God is steady and never absent.

What is it that sustains the awakened woman? You probably have your own list. The list I invite you to consider includes: silence, beauty, friendship, family, community and nature. These sustaining powers are intimately connected and overlap in our lives.

Silence: A Treasure and a Challenge

At first glance, silence may seem more challenging than supportive. However, silence is necessary to hear the heartbeat of God, to notice the Spirit when and wherever it is present, which, of course, is everywhere. In our noisy, fast-paced world, silence is rare, precious and essential. When my sister's many children were preschoolers, she told me that her only time alone came when she was in the shower. Though I laughed at the time, she let me know that the water spraying over her made her grateful to God for this time, and that she prayed in that shower for the many needs of her growing family. Can you imagine how God the Mother smiled on that chosen mystical moment?

The pace and sounds of our culture practically disallow silence as a value and even less as a necessity of life. And yet contemplative activities, those pauses to become aware of what is going on inside of us and around us offer a chance to reflect. Reflection is what weaves awareness of the presence and wisdom of God into our actions, decisions and relationships. In those reflective pauses, we can go a bit deeper, notice a yearning, a thing of beauty, a question that needs to be asked, our own deep soul where Life and Spirit abide. A person of great wisdom, Raimon Pannikar, writes that, "Silence alone offers a space for freedom: God is freedom and silence is the 'space' needed for experiencing God."[7] Such times, even short times, of silence sustain a woman with the courage to be wide awake amidst personal and global challenge, and even disaster.

Beauty: A Gift That Saves Us

Beauty not only sustains us. It has the capability of saving us from despair and from wanting to close our eyes in the face of difficulty. A reason to be awake is to not miss the beauty. Without denying ugliness and even the destructive aspect of nature, the beauty of creation and of gifts which flow from the creative minds and hearts of human beings are astounding in their power to sustain and uplift.

With awareness of earth's wounds and fragility because of our misuse, we awaken anew to her beauty. Awareness of the earth as magnificent gift is flowering among scientists, poets, spiritual seekers and even political leaders across the world. Jesus used the mustard seed, the lilies of the field, living water, the sower and the seed, the birds of the air and other creation images to communicate his understanding of God and sacredness in life. The medieval mystics grounded their mystical sensibilities in a theology of creation.[8] Jesus' theology of creation, if you will, and creation itself sustained those awakened by his message. In addition to creation itself, great works of art, beautiful pieces of sculpture or clothing, someone's smile, a well-crafted story, and, of course, the kindergarten masterpieces on the refrigerator door are all small miracles for the sustenance of life.

Relationships: The Heart of Women's Spirituality

The sustaining force of friendship, family and community is also vital. How many stories have you heard in which relationships between and among women have literally made it possible to go on? Perhaps you have experienced this yourself. Mothers who have lost sons or daughters in war have come together to support one another. Women who met in college and continue to get together year after year into old age, count on and celebrate one another. Women lay down their lives for family and community. They are also supported by those families and communities when they take risks or experience loss. For women, at the heart of everything is relationship. It is hard to overestimate the significance of our relationships in the journey toward being spiritually awake.

The exquisite aspects of life, its devastating dimensions and its incredible possibilities are enfolded in the prayer of an awakened woman. "We wake, if we ever wake at all," Annie Dillard writes, "to mystery, rumours of death, beauty, violence."[9] A decision to allow myself to become more awake, more conscious of the peace life offers is serious and significant. It is serious because you will find shadow as well as light in yourself. You will be aware of the consequences of war and the struggle for peace. You will weep at what women suffer in poverty and from violence, and work to change it. You will taste dryness in prayer and also sense the meaning of presence and boundless Love. This decision is significant because being human, being a child of God, being a reflective member of the universe, being a cocreator with the Divine of your own spiritual journey, invites you to choose to be fully alive (see Deuteronomy 30:19–20 and John 10:10). Already you know much of the seriousness and significance of awakening. However, because it is a lifelong process, the choice is always before us.

And so, tomorrow morning when the alarm goes off or the baby cries or the motel phone rings with the wake-up call, or the sun is bright—awaken. Once the shock that sleeping time is over passes, you could choose to pray this prayer:

Oh, my dear God —
I choose to be awake today
to all that is.
I open my eyes, my heart,
my whole being to this day.
I will receive the beauty and trouble
the day holds.
And, yes, my dear Companion,
I will care for myself.
Surely, I will find you
along the way since you
are in every single cell giving life and love.
I awaken. I trust.

FOOD FOR THOUGHT

1. How would you have to change to see yourself as one radically amazed or willing to hold the world in your arms?
2. What is it in your personal life or in the global reality that tempts you to choose "sleeping" over awakening?
3. Are you convinced that you have mystic sensibilities—that you can know God through your own experience? Why or why not? Do you have a story of noticing the mystic within yourself?

RITUAL

1. For this ritual, it would be helpful to place before you: an alarm clock, a bright cloth (a "wake-up" color) and three to five rocks or stones.
2. Light a candle with the prayer: "May the Light of the Universe awaken us this day."
3. Place the stones on the table and hold your hands over them in silent blessing. You can let each stone symbolize an event, a moment in your life that really woke you up—something beautiful, a crisis, a spiritual awareness, a community experience, a time of intimacy with nature or another person.
4. Reflect in silence on each of those events as you hold the stone you've chosen to symbolize the experience. If you are in a group, each person may wish to share one of her experiences. If you are alone, you may wish to write one or all of the experiences in a journal. You may wish to end in silence or say the prayer at the end of this chapter or create a prayer of your own.

CHAPTER THREE

• THIRSTING •

Desire is one of the most important elements of the spiritual life. It is the fuel, the "eros," the Spirit-power that enables us to reach out to God, each other and the world. [1]

—Elizabeth A. Dreyer

Are you moved by Spirit-power to reach out to God, to all creatures, to the world? Now that we have explored the landscape within you and the vast complex world around you, has a stirring—even a small one—happened in your soul? You might name that stirring "longing" or "desiring," both of which hold an important place in the prayer traditions of the world's religions. Saint Augustine's famous lines about human hearts being restless until they rest in God imply a desire to move toward God as our home or resting place. According to the mystical traditions, our authentic erotic desires, our deep longings and our great thirsts are given to us by God and lead to God. And, oh happy truth, God also longs for and desires us. Mechtilde of Magdeburg hears God saying to her soul, "I desired you before the world began. / I desire you now / as you desire me."[2]

While all the strength and depth of longing and desiring are included in the dimension of the spiritual life I want to address in this chapter, I choose the word *thirsting*. A moving translation of the opening lines of Psalm 63 helps to explain my choice:

O God, you are my God, I seek you,
   my soul thirsts for you;
my flesh faints for you,
   as in a dry and weary land where there is no water.
(Psalms 63:1)

Thirst is a powerful human experience. It is concrete and familiar. The infant instinctively finds its mother's breast to quench its thirst; a very old woman I know thirsts for death to quench her thirst for life. Right now large numbers of human beings need water and die for lack of it. Can we believe that the human soul can thirst for the Divine as the parched earth and her creatures yearn for water?

In a poignant moment in a Gospel story, Jesus uses the word "thirst." When Jesus dares to speak to the Samaritan woman in a Gospel story, his first words are, "Give me a drink" (John 4:7). The entire encounter can be seen as a mutual quenching of thirst through open dialogue, respect and, if you will, an exchange of "living water." When Jesus was on the cross, according to the Gospels, he needed water but was given instead vinegar to drink. Jesus' thirst was not quenched. Neither Jesus, nor anyone, can live without water. It is a worthwhile venture to name and attend to the thirsts within us and to discover that the thirst for our deepest selves, peace on our earth, justice for the vulnerable and for Sacred Presence are intimately related. For what does your soul ardently thirst? John O'Donohue, a poetic Irish writer, speaks of longing or spiritual thirst as taking you toward the "absolute realization of all the possibilities that sleep in the clay of your heart."[3] To take steps in this direction, this realization of possibilities, let us assume a degree of thirst for God, for the Divine, in every one of us. If the stirring in one's soul moves us to pray, who or what is the God we address in prayer?

God Beyond All Names
More than likely, it has been a long time since any of us has imagined the Divine as a top manager, satisfier of requests, a rescuer, a fixer or a

parent who tells us what to do. And yet sometimes remnants of those labels for God slip into the minds of mature praying women. More likely, though, the thought of God as distant other or demander of servile obedience does pop up in the middle of a peaceful meditation or a careful discernment. None of these understandings of God, the Holy One, hinted at in the last few sentences have a place in a spiritually mature relationship with God. Rather, such a relationship involves the experience of deep and inclusive love. It involves letting go of unhelpful images and understandings of God.

It is actually very good news that no one can define or precisely name God. This theological reality is not a startling postmodern theory. Theologians have long described God as unfathomable Mystery. Karl Rahner, renowned German theologian of the twentieth century, called God "incomprehensible Holy Mystery."[4] Augustine readily acknowledged that God has no gender, and yet gender-specific God language abounds. Though gender-specific God language still abounds in the worship and written prayers of numerous faith traditions, the truth that God is very large indeed, beyond all images and metaphors, is finally available to all God's people. Contemporary women theologians and some men are releasing the Sacred Presence from the limits previous mindsets have imposed.

It is as magnificent a realization as it is profound to proclaim from the mountaintops that God is unfathomable Mystery. By referring to the Divine in this way, spiritual writers are opening what seemed closed, widening what seemed narrow, freeing what seemed captive to the perspectives of a few. Yes, we need to name God, yet, at the same time, we can calmly assert that human naming always fails to encompass Mystery in its fullness.

Whenever I teach a class or give a talk about God, I begin with a piece of music. It is called "Mystery" and it is from Paul Winter's "Missa Gaia," a Mass in celebration of Mother Earth. It is a solo rendered in a full, rich woman's voice. If you were not stirred to thirst for

Divine Mystery before the song, the music would certainly invite you to open your whole self to the Sacred. I want to share a few of the words that capture the wonder and power of Mystery:

> You are alive. . .
> You are the Fire in my heart;
> You are the Holy Sound.
> You are all of Life—It is to you I sing.
> The song speaks of God living. . .
> in the seed of a tree
> in the wind as it blows
> in the laughter of children
> and also in the sun, planets and stars.[5]

Long ago I learned from the writings of Thomas Aquinas, a thirteenth-century theologian, that the whole universe participates in divine goodness and represents it better than any single being ever could. The song "Mystery" expresses that truth in twentieth-century language. Language for the Divine is mediated through what is going on in our world.

The God Who Is More Than We Can Imagine

The world in which we do our thinking and praying vibrates with the rapidity and immensity of changes which impact our experience of God, ourselves and the universe. Three ideas that are opening theological and spiritual doors right now are renewed and widespread awareness of the Divine as beyond all names, an evolutionary perspective on life, and seeing anew the interconnectedness of all things.

Mystery

The incomprehensibility of God is most helpful in the effort to expand language about the Divine. Raimon Panikkar has written a book that reads like a mystical hymn to the namelessness of God. Panikkar is well-known for his work on world religions. He insists that no discourse can describe Divine Mystery.[6] A number of contemporary women theologians also write in celebration of God's incomprehensibility. Beyond images and metaphors, unlimited, large beyond imaginings, open to the fullest possible range of forms—these phrases hint at what I see as a type of delighting in and being awed by Mystery. This reawakening takes the conversation about the God for whom we thirst far beyond changing pronouns or adding "Mother" to the Our Father. Rather, this emphasis on Mystery moves us to a new spiritual world where countless "icons" are welcome, as long as no one of them claims to express all that Sacred Presence is.

Evolutionary Perspective

The Divine Spirit is and has been living and moving in continuously new ways for billions of years in this universe. To pay attention to this movement now is to embrace an evolutionary perspective. It was not too surprising to find in a recent issue of the journal *What Is Enlightenment?* that a group of women who have been working together for twelve years on the issue of consciousness, chose as number one on a list of ten challenges for a conscious and liberated woman, "Holding an evolutionary perspective."[7]

An evolutionary perspective keeps alive the belief that movement toward wholeness is in process. Birth and death, construction and destruction are and have been part of that process for more than fifteen billion years. Our prayer is grounded in the truth that the Divine Presence has been intimately involved in that entire creating process. We too are a part of this evolutionary process. It is often said that human beings are the universe become conscious of itself. Each of us is a microcosm of the evolutionary process of the entire universe. I have a little book called *The Hand of God: Thoughts and Images Reflecting the Spirit of the Universe.* The colored pictures in it are from the Hubble telescope; the quotations are from scientific, poetic and spiritual thinkers of our time. The book's images reveal gifts of the evolutionary process in the stars, planets, galaxies and moons pictured. It is no wonder that we thirst for relationships with the Mystery involved with this incredible creation.

Interconnectedness

Long ago, Thomas Merton said in one of his talks to novices that the contemplative sees the interconnectedness of all things. One thing that seems true of the evolution of consciousness is that it is on a very slow track. Only now, fifty or sixty years after Merton's comment and centuries after the mystics prayed with that same awareness, has the mark of interconnectedness become integral to contemporary spiritual thought.

Mary Grey, an English theologian, speaks of "knowing ourselves as part of the web of life in communion with and interdependent with all living things."[8] The "web of life" is an effective image for interconnectedness. Panikkar writes of God being so interior to the world that there is no way we can separate God from the world.[9] It is not a giant step from these insights to an awareness of the sacredness of the earth and all living things and, perhaps, to a new understanding of "life to the full" (John 10:10). It does take a contemplative look, a long, loving look at the real, to grasp the beauty and the challenge of interconnectedness. When you acknowledge a thirst for God, does this Sacred Presence connect you with all living things?

These characteristics of an emerging spirituality, of a thirst for the divine in today's world are not new; however, they have not been prevalent in mainstream Christian spirituality. God as incomprehensible Mystery, an evolutionary perspective and the interconnectedness of all things are positive contributions to women's spiritualities and our prayer lives. These characteristics have not always been emphasized. Thus, it is important to address aspects of theology and spirituality that have been damaging to women.

Too Limited a God Image

"Who [or what] will separate us from the love of Christ?" (Romans 8:35). This passage goes on to name wild and threatening things and then boldly asserts that, in fact, not anything can separate us from God and God's love. You may want to say, as I do, that certain things over the centuries of religious development have pushed women toward the edge of belonging, if not separation. A system that has prevailed in society has prevailed in our church, and that is a system of domination and hierarchical dualism. For many centuries, the prevalent image of God was that of a sovereign male demanding and distant, possibly frightening and judgmental, definitely patriarchal. Unfathomable Mystery was recreated by the culture into the image I have just described, and in many church circles around the globe, that patriarchal image prevails to this day.

Though it is clear that movement toward interconnectedness and oneness is emerging in a forceful way in today's spiritual world, dualism has done its harmful work. In a system in which the "rules" say that spirit is valued over matter, humanity over nature, heaven over earth, soul over body and man over woman, it is nearly impossible to celebrate equality and thirst for relationship with a God who reigns supreme over all of it. The spiritual teachings embedded in this patriarchal tradition have affected women negatively in their spiritual lives.

Marvelous women theologians, thinkers, prayers and activists have discovered and created fissures in these dominant systems. Through those fissures, the living water of women's hard work is springing forth. Revisioning and birthing is ongoing in the world of women's spirituality. Many women in midlife or later years are still healing from the silencing, subjugation and excessive self-sacrifice. Happily, this difficult process is going on steadily and thoroughly. Younger women and girls just entering into a conscious life of the Spirit are in search of those streams of living water—and many are finding them.

Allow me to share, with her permission, a life-changing prayer experience of a woman who is now ninety-six years old. She studied some theology when she was in her forties, long before any significant fissures opened up in the established patriarchal system in society or church. Her custom was to engage in a kind of dialogic prayer with one member of the Trinity or another. One night in her prayer, she asked Jesus if she, like saints that preceded her, might exchange hearts with him. She wanted to love the world with his very heart. Jesus replied, "Yes," and, in some mysterious way gave her his heart. She was happy beyond imagining and went about her work and her life filled with new awareness of the love and life of the Spirit of Christ in her. However, that was not the end of this experience. Several nights later, Jesus was once again present in her prayer. He asked her to return his heart and he would give her heart back to her. She felt hurt, utterly disappointed, and pleaded with Jesus to let her keep his heart. Then she heard Jesus speak:

> You need to reclaim
> your own heart, my dear one,
> your woman's heart.
> That is because what the world needs especially right now
> is a woman's way of loving, and that I,
> Jesus, cannot do.

That was in 1981, and this woman has since then been studying, praying and intuiting her woman's way to channel God's love to the world.

I include this story at the end of the section on woman-dominating aspects of Christian spirituality and theology because the story holds relevant truths for us. First, God is not limited by systems in God's relationship with any one of us. Another truth is that we have mystics in our time. The third truth is that each person has a unique way of praying and that no method, no particular words are the "right" or "only" ones. And lastly, the authenticity, sincerity and wisdom of this woman invite me, and perhaps you, to hear her prayer and take it to heart.

We need to bid farewell to the norm of an exclusively male image of God and to the "little patriarch" that lives in each of us because we have been so immersed in this system of subjugation. The phrase "a woman's work is never done" applies here. We can and need to allow new images, understandings, characteristics of the God to whom we pray and for whom we thirst, bubble up in us. It is a birthing time in each of us and in our world so in need of healing and of new ways of being together in the Spirit. It is *always* a birthing time.

Moving through life in a spiritually healthy way requires constant vigilance about when it is time to let go of one way of thinking, praying, relating and, when it is time, to encourage the seed of new ways of perceiving to grow. I can remember the time and place when it was clear that I had let go of an exclusively male God image. And yet I had not yet found a new image or understanding of God to which I might relate. That situation was incredibly uncomfortable. I describe it as being in a state of suspension. Now I see that time as a turning point that completely changed and enriched my spiritual life. The seed growing within me was that of the many names for God and the transformative power of these names.

The God of Countless Names

Before I invite you to revisit some of the names and understandings of the divine in the Hebrew and Christian Scriptures, I want to repeat that our vocabulary is inadequate. All descriptors and analogies fall short in the face of the Holy One, Divine Mystery. The human search for names for God in every religious tradition, in every corner of the globe, in every century since humans have inhabited the earth, has been integral to our nature. And yet, the incomprehensibility of God remains. We humans can never pin God down, and that fact frees God and us from a limiting and narrow focus.

Names for God count. A warrior God can be used to justify killing and demonizing enemies. A patriarchal God can be used to justify the subjugation of women and children. An abusive God can be used to justify victimization of the innocent. A judging God can be used to justify a lack of forgiveness. Would you choose to pray to any of the Gods thus imaged? Would you choose to contemplate, to be in close relationship with, to trust and count on these images of God?

The qualities for God which are named above are familiar and have had their time and place in every major faith. Because that is true, we have a need, as individuals and as a human race, for the healing of our image and understanding of God. Evidence abounds in relationships among individuals and nations that negative perceptions of God contribute to escalations of religious wars, abusive treatment of women across the globe, power being used to oppress people and the creation of empires. It is time to look closely at the relationship of Jesus with his *Abba*, at the intimate relationship of well-known mystics with their God and at our own tastes of the Spirit as source and presence of love.

The Bible is a primary source for imagery about God. Nature images include rock, burning bush, eagle's wings, running streams and many more. Personal imagery is also plentiful—protector, nurturer, mother, father, shepherd, guardian. Through the centuries, some of these images have been held up and promoted and others have been deemphasized, even hidden. Women theologians, preachers and prayers have been finding and raising up those hidden images over the past several centuries. Rebecca Jackson, a nineteenth-century African American preacher, discovered in her own prayer "a Mother in the Deity." She called this meeting a "new scene" that she needed to believe in and about which she had to preach. Weeping, she told of her gladness to have a Mother, "and though they never heard it before, I was made able by Her Holy Spirit of Wisdom to make it so plain that a child could understand it."[10] What a great moment for Rebecca Jackson and for the sisterhood of women, ourselves among them, who rejoice to know we have a Mother in the Deity.

Another strong biblical image of God is Sophia. Sophia has emerged as a significant female dimension of the Divine. *Sophia*, the Greek personification of "wisdom," has her roots in the goddess tradition; however, she is a real biblical personage and a very powerful one as can be seen in these passages. Enjoy these examples of Sophia's invigorating, delightful and engaging personality:

For she is a reflection of eternal light,
a spotless mirror of the working of God,
and an image of [God's] goodness. (Wisdom 7:26)

...she is easily discerned by those who love her,
and is found by those who seek her.
...she goes about seeking those worthy of her,
...
and meets them in every thought. (Wisdom 6:12, 16)

therefore walk in the way of the good,
    and keep to the paths of the just. (Proverbs 2:20)

...in every generation, she passes into holy souls
and makes them friends of God, and prophets. (Wisdom 7:27)

She is more beautiful than the sun
and excels every constellation of the stars. (Wisdom 7:29)

These passages reveal a being full of vitality and reflective of all a woman would want to find in the Divine. Sophia presents herself in Proverbs, but also in Wisdom, Baruch and Sirach—books omitted from Protestant versions of the Bible. She is assertive, angry, creative, energetic and confident. In the book of Baruch (see Baruch 3:27–35), Sophia is hidden and God is in search of her. Only when God finds her does creation begin. She was "beside [God], like a master worker; / and...daily his delight, / rejoicing before him always / ... / and delighting in the human race" (Proverbs 8:30–31). Throughout Scripture, Sophia identifies herself as sister, mother, female beloved, chef and hostess, establisher of justice and spunky woman. For various reasons, Sophia was repressed and all but disappeared from Western theological thinking. The time has come to bring her back, and women who have studied the Wisdom literature and Sophia are doing just that.

We have often seen pictures of Michelangelo's beautiful painting of the creation of Adam which is on the ceiling of the Sistine Chapel in the Vatican. The focus is often on the outstretched arm of the great God figure reaching and touching the finger of the male human figure. What is seldom seen is God's other arm. That arm embraces a beautiful woman also engaged in the process of creation. Who could she be other than Sophia herself?

Throughout these first chapters, I have emphasized that God is incomprehensible and unfathomable. No description is adequate. Yet in our humanness we seek symbols that point to something beyond ourselves, and to whom we can relate. Though the debate on the interpretation of Sophia continues, her theological and spiritual significance are undeniable. The work of Elizabeth Johnson makes a tremendous contribution in bringing Sophia out of the shadows and into the light. She concludes that Sophia's actions in creation and in redeeming are divine and that Sophia is a "female personification of God's own being in creative and saving involvement with the world."[11] Does your thirst for God move you to further explore relationship with Sophia? Our tradition gifts us with Sophia and other biblical images; the mystics also offer a plethora of images for the Sacred Presence.

A prominent image and understanding of the Divine in the Christian tradition is the Trinity. We find language, images and understandings of this Mystery compatible with the consciousness of this historical moment emerging, particularly among women theologians. In another volume in this series, Elizabeth Dreyer writes about the Trinity as a community of love. She invites us to make the image of the Trinity precious and inspiring rather than regarding it simply as an unexplainable theological construct or three Persons with three tasks. The Trinity, so long a part of the Christian tradition, is being seen anew through the eyes of contemporary women theologians. This gift of new vision broadens not only our ways of perceiving the Divine but also our way of praying. How does the image of God as a community of love influence your prayer? In addition to the images of God found in our tradition, yet seen in a new way, entirely new images are arising out of women's experience around the globe and in this historical moment. In the next section, we attend to the importance of women's contemporary experience.

The Face of God as You See It

"The whole of life lies in the verb 'seeing,'" writes Teilhard de Chardin, a twentieth-century mystic and theologian. I couldn't agree more. When your experience is that of seeing the very face of God in some way, that affects the way you perceive your own life and the world. When you share your own naming of Sacred Presence, you gift the world with one more fragment of the great mystery we call God.

Women hesitate to trust their own experience of God, especially if it doesn't match commonly held images and understandings. It is especially difficult to share experiences of God that are discomforting or alienating. Once someone hesitatingly shared with me in hushed tones that the image of God that best expressed her experience was a block of ice. She thought she was off the spiritual path to have that image so prominent in her prayer. Her honesty and willingness to stay with that image brought her to valuable insights about continued presence and about what causes ice to melt. Even the image of a block of ice helps open the great Mystery of life in and with the Spirit of God. When we realize we can trust our experience, creative, imaginative and profound images and questions and understandings emerge.

One source of encouragement to trust our own experiences of God comes from women who have gone before us and those who live among us who have shared what they have seen. Theologian and writer Elizabeth Schussler Fiorenza names God "creative darkness" and "liberating strength" in a prayer that she wrote. Brazilian theologian Ivone Gebara has spoken of the way desperately poor women in her country speak of God. They see God as "the last resort," "the ally when no daily bread is available," "the one who wants the world to be just." God is

immediate and necessary to these Brazilian women, not always comforting or thirst-quenching.

Ordinary women like us who pray, thirst and have begun to share
images and understandings of God offer new ways of seeing and hope.
Some words about God experience that I have heard recently are these:

Who are you, God?
   great energy, sparking the flame of life connecting all beings
   the center of a circle of belonging.
God is the main character in my book of life.
I am wondering about God as energy. I am feeling a need to
visualize God with many face shapes; skin colors; statures and
races.
God, the one who doesn't solve my problems.
God is the great within of all that is.
God is the small, old woman on the bus with a bouquet of
flowers in her hand.
God, an unreasonable lover who turns my running into danc-
ing.
God, the one whom I fear will ask too much.
God, extravagant and loving, seen in people around us and in
the earth.

Women thirst for a relationship with the living God that connects with
their struggles, dreams and hopes. In the names for God listed above,
vitality, fear, wonder, intimacy, disappointment, questioning and sim-
plicity are expressed. Not any one experience is definitive; each is
authentic and valuable. Only you have the glimpse of God that emerges
in your prayer.

The glimpse of God you have, whether it is filled with consolation
or longing, suffering or near despair, is a source of strength for the community of praying women in the world. It is a source of strength to me
that the women of Brazil see God as an ally when there is no bread. It

makes me smile that someone's running turns into dancing through God's presence. It touches me that the small, old woman with the flowers reveals God's face to someone. What glimpse of God is yours? For what do you thirst in this phase of your life?

Thirst for God is as common among women of faith as thirst for cool, clear water is among all people. In this chapter, the intent is to invite praying women to notice their own thirst and what might be "living water" for us. If opening ourselves to God is a way to quench our spiritual thirst, what would make us want to do that? Relationship with a God who is love and brings life can move us to be open, even to seek relationship. An obstacle to that relationship could be an image of God that is alienating. The work of this chapter is to point out the existence of this obstacle and to invite you to consider God as Incomprehensible Mystery and to see the many possible "faces of God."

Our thirsting for God is never over because Holy Mystery has more fullness of life than we can ever hold and because our human longing never ends. God with any face invites us to more life. Whether you are in a time of suffering or joy, interior war or peace, feeling weak or courageous—you thirst and God is with you. Faith, hope and friends offer us water even in times of drought—especially then. They are in those times God's very face.

FOOD FOR THOUGHT

1. No matter how old you are, spend a few minutes remembering how you understood or imaged God as a small child, as a teenager, as a young adult, at midlife and beyond. Write these images in a journal and note next to each one a quality of the Divine.

2. Do you have a memory of an experience, a teaching, a liturgical celebration that moved you to long for God—even to thirst for relationship with God? If possible, share that experience with another person.

RITUAL

1. Gather four or five small candles, a long necklace or a piece of yarn or colored thread and a song—from a CD (the companion CD to this series offers some wonderful choices) or hymnal or one you know from memory—that speaks to you of the mystery of God. (The song doesn't need to be a hymn.)

2. When the ritual space is prepared, sing or play the song you chose. After the song, pause in silence for a minute or two. Light the candles. Light one candle naming your image of God as a child; repeat this action for the image of God you had as a teenager, a young adult, a mature woman. With the four candles lighted in front of you, reflect on the question, "What is it for which I thirst right now in my spiritual life?" If you are working with a group, share your responses with one another, if you wish.

3. Take your necklace or thread and weave it around your candles, a sign of the movement of the Spirit throughout your life. As you do so, describe the way you see and understand God now.

4. Pray:

   O Mystery, your names are many and sacred. On this day, I pray in thanksgiving for your presence when I was a child and throughout my life. Heal any wounds in me, those I love, all peoples, wounds caused by false understandings of you, O God. Awaken in me, I ask you, a great thirst for You, O loving, nonviolent, just and compassionate Mystery.

5. Close with the song you chose.

CHAPTER FOUR

• STRUGGLING •

*Weeping women, women whose hearts moan like a flute because
those they love have come to harm, are everywhere in the world. As*
imago Dei *(image of God) they point to the mystery of divine sorrow, of an unimaginable compassionate God who suffers with
beloved creation. ...If God grieves with them in the middle of disaster, then there may yet be a way forward.*[1]

—Elizabeth A. Johnson

Not many women who read this chapter will be unfamiliar with its focus—
struggling. No day goes by that doesn't hold some awareness and experience of life's various struggles—personal, familial, national and global.
Today, as I began to write this chapter, the phone rang with news of the
death of a friend, Diane, who had been living with ovarian cancer for
three years. She was fifty years old. Of course I put down my pen and
went immediately to the hospice care center where the family was gathering for a final good-bye and prayer.

As I continue writing a few days later, Diane's life of struggle and
triumph—joy, pain and sadness—and her courage in the face of those
realities moves through my mind like a fine film in slow motion. She
chose two of Anne Sexton's poems entitled "Rowing" and "The Rowing
Endeth" which I read at her memorial service. The second poem
begins, "I'm mooring my rowboat / at the dock of an island called
God."[2] I see that line as a prayer of confidence and faith. It is a great

line to describe the conclusion of a life replete with struggle and rooted in God.

The consideration of struggle as part of our spiritual lives and a place from which we pray raises again the question explored in the last chapter, "Who is the God of our prayer?" In the end, will you be moved to moor your "rowboat at the dock of an island called God?" You will be far more likely to do so if you are convinced of the truth that God, who loves life, does not will suffering for people. God desires happiness for us. Though God gets blamed for both personal suffering and natural disasters, the Holy One is not guilty. We are familiar with the sayings "suffering is good for the soul"; "no pain, no gain"; and the unhelpful words often voiced in the face of tragedy, "This is God's will." The memory of this line in John's Gospel is a mantra for protection against the idea of God wanting death-dealing experiences for us: "I came that they may have life, and have it abundantly" (John 10:10). If we image God as Mother, Father, Friend, Compassionate One, we can see God as weeping with us as we face the inevitable struggles of life. A secret of the cross of Christ is that we do not suffer alone.

This chapter is called "struggling" rather than "suffering" because it is inclusive of the everyday things that are definitely difficult but are not quite what we normally call suffering. Things like the demands of parenting preschool children, the effort required for communication in an intimate relationship, economic struggles in a family—the list goes on. Such experiences are integral to living a spiritual life and have a valid place in our prayer. Yet we may be reluctant to name them suffering unless they are experienced to an extreme degree. "Sometimes human suffering is dramatic and horrifying. More often it is ordinary, humble and quiet."[3]

This chapter will address ordinary and radical life struggles and the part they play in our prayer and spiritual lives. Julian of Norwich writes, "For I tell you, howsoever you do, you shall have woe." We may not thank Julian for this insight; however, we don't have to live very long before we nod in agreement. Julian and so many spiritual writers, while conscious of the negative aspects of suffering and struggling, also see that they can lead people to encounters with God, to compassion for others in need, and to the will to reach out in support.

You may be moved, as I am, to ponder questions like these:

- How could a forty-three-year-old woman who has six children and is suddenly widowed cope and even become happy and spiritually mature?
- How did Paula D'Arcy survive the accident which took the life of her husband and three-year-old child and become a woman full of spiritual vitality?
- How could a young woman participate in the recovery of human remains from mass graves in Guatemala and return with deeper faith and fierce commitment to God and God's people?
- How does a woman who was physically harmed and then thrown out of her home at age ten become a successful professor of theology and a deeply spiritual person?

These questions are about "ordinary" women who have found a way to respond to serious struggle through prayer and faith. Each is a living witness to the fact that the struggles of life, even great struggles and suffering, need not destroy us. The suffering in these instances was horrible. Yet someplace deep within each of these women was a life force, a power, courage, prayer that was stronger than that suffering.

Daily Struggles

After pondering such dramatic struggles, let us step back and reflect on those called "ordinary, humble and quiet." In every phase of a woman's life these challenges are evident. At first, you may see little connection between the kind of struggles named here and prayer and spirituality. And yet if we believe that life experience is revelatory, then all of our lives have the potential to speak to us of God. If you are a student, do you struggle with grades, roommates, pleasing teachers, being honest or a failed computer? If you are a mother, do you struggle with getting up when the baby cries at night, or with feeling isolated because you are confined, or with feeling as though your life really isn't your own? As a professional woman, do you struggle with unfair pay scales, domineering employers, poor treatment in the workplace or conflict with colleagues? As an aging woman, do you struggle with your mind playing tricks, with the absence of energy, with the death of friends? Surely you could make your own list of daily struggles.

In the face of life's "lemons," we are given an opportunity to respond in a variety of ways. Noticing and being awake are tools that can help us relate life and prayer. We have the chance to see the big and small deaths in daily life in new ways related to the paschal mystery that is at the heart of Christian spirituality. The student striving for *A*s needs to notice her unreal expectations of herself and "die" to those. Could it be that the mother who is isolated needs to "die" a bit to her independence and call a friend for help? Is it possible that the professional woman can let go of a tendency to conform and summon the courage to confront the injustice in her workplace? Does the older woman have to "die" to her deeply entrenched work ethic and accept her limits? In other words, it is possible to frame the struggles of daily life in a spiritual context. This involves noticing our disappointment, embarrassment, frustration—even honoring them. Looking at struggle as a reflection of the paschal mystery in our faith and in the universe involves having compassion for ourselves as God has compassion for us. We can try not to shut down, and instead open ourselves up to what is going on within us and around us. While we may be tempted to escape these daily struggles, at times we can find the courage within to look right into their face.

The Spirit may also invite us beyond ourselves, to the larger struggles and greater deaths all around us. Looking into the face of our own exhaustion and lack of comfort might bring to our minds and hearts the exiled mothers in refugee camps comforting their children.

Compassion arises and we send it "on the wings of the Spirit" to our sisters across the globe. And so, with deep respect for our own reality and open to the gift of compassion from our loving God, we can also channel that compassion and touch the death experience of others' suffering. This very process holds the promise of new life, of resurrection. Out of the experience of our daily life struggles, we might pray:

> "Compassionate One, I come to you today just as I am. I bring the frustration and struggle life brought to me this day. Because of the way you care for me and bless me, I honor my struggle and ask your help to have compassion for myself and all the struggling women of the world. Amen."

Midlife and the Search for Meaning

Although the struggle at midlife is an ordinary and expected life passage, I include a brief section on it here because it can be excruciatingly painful. It can also be a particularly significant time in the spiritual life. As many of you know, the midlife passage usually comes somewhere between the ages of forty-five and fifty-five. It is ordinarily a time of great transition in life. Changes occur in our bodies and energy level; some consider retiring; illness is more common; career change may be on the horizon; children begin leaving home; and the possibility of being a grandparent or a mentor presents itself. These transitions often raise the question, "What is the real meaning of life itself?"

Sometimes this rite of passage is described as a crisis of meaning since those going through it often wonder if there really is much meaning to life. It is a spiritually significant time because we are presented with a crossroads—to choose relationship with the divine and a spiritual path, or not. Angeles Arrien speaks and writes extensively about the second half of life. She says that the main task of midlife is to integrate "the two threads of one's life, the within and the without."[4] While that is a simple statement, the experience often involves a very difficult struggle. This passage definitely requires new eyes with which to see the world and a kind of fearlessness as the ground trembles beneath you. In my own life, this passage involved a serious vocational crisis and a drastic shift in my image and understanding of God. The process includes staying with confusion, brokenheartedness, a sense of hopelessness and uncertainty.

That said, the movement is also toward freedom, depth and integrity. You are led where you would rather not go. However, you and God cocreate a more authentic self. This happens by facing what is hidden in yourself—the gold and the dross—by finding time for reflection and silence and time in nature. It is often a time when women begin to make retreats, seek spiritual guidance, form faith-sharing circles and develop an interest in reading spiritual books. Creativity takes center stage and some women begin painting, sculpting and dancing. Relationships change and we are "challenged to make the passage from loving, serving, 'being with,' because of the pleasure and joy it gives us, to loving and serving regardless of the cost."[5] For believers, God may have an important part to play in this relational change which leads us to a more committed love.

Moving through such uncertainty liberates us. We no longer see aging as only negative or debilitating, but realize that it also opens the way for the mature vitality seen in Rosa Parks, Nelson Mandela and, perhaps, our own parents and grandparents. Through this sometimes chaotic passage, we are being transformed by grace. We learn determination and openness to become more fully the people we are meant to be. The midlife struggle authenticates the unique footprint that you are. Out of our experience of midlife struggle, we might pray this:

"God, life is nearly impossible. It tastes like dust in my mouth. Where are you? Who are you? What I thought was important has no meaning now. Where am I going? I am trying to trust you. Only raw faith connects me to you, a thin thread of hope. Help me. Amen."

Grief and Loss

No matter how deeply we believe in peace and life beyond death, the loss of a loved one brings us to our knees. Two vivid images from Scripture move us to awareness of the meaning of grief. One is Jesus at the tomb of his dear friend Lazarus, where, the verse tells us, "Jesus began to weep" (John 11:35). The word for *wept* in Greek indicates a kind of weeping that causes one to double over. The other image is that of Mary receiving the body of the dead Jesus in her arms. This image is forever memorialized in Michelangelo's sculpture of the Pietá. Any woman who has lost a child and anyone who has lost a very close friend or a spouse knows that there are no words. Actually, Jesus' almost-collapsed body at Lazarus's death and Mary's great receptive lap holding her beloved son speak well the depth and anguish of the response.

While death is a normal part of life, it certainly doesn't feel normal to a person grieving. We are often totally unprepared for the impact of death and for the long grieving that follows. Grief is not an illness that requires a cure; rather, it is a call to embark on a journey of the soul. The emptiness within, which can never be filled, is a space created by the depth of love for the person lost in death. In a lecture on companioning a grieving person, Alan Wofelt said, "[T]he grief journey requires contemplation (that long, loving look) and turning inward. In other words, it requires depression, anxiety and loss of control. It requires going to the wilderness."[6] It is frightening to be in this wilderness and to think we should not be feeling depressed, anxious, out of control or in pain. Actually, it is a comfort to know that these feelings and experiences are a part of the spiritual journey that the death of a loved one occasions. Eventually, with the help of family, friends, faith and time, we experience movement toward living with the changes brought about by the loss of a loved one. It takes time, isn't easy and is certainly a spiritual struggle and challenge.

A similar wilderness faces us when we experience illness, divorce and other losses related to the one we face in death. It is very difficult to pray in this wilderness when we can no longer sense God's presence, feel alone, are unable to pray and even wonder if we have any faith left at all. But this journey is an important part of our spirituality. It is a time to hold on to the truth that the Spirit is somehow with you and that you will indeed survive. Death and serious illness tear us open. But from that forcibly opened heart, healing is possible and new life will come. Praying in the midst of intense grief involves endurance, getting through the day, breathing in spite of fear, allowing time for tears, calling out in anguish and accepting yourself just as you are on a given day. In your aloneness, imagine, if you are able, the God who weeps with you enfolding you in a blanket or cloak named compassion.

Radical Suffering

The kind of struggles and suffering I have described thus far are experiences all of us meet in life. These struggles are places in which we grow and change. They are integral to our spiritual lives. In addition to these daily challenges, there is radical suffering. In her book *Women and the Value of Suffering*, Kristine Rankka defines radical suffering as the suffering of the innocent which is unmerited and debilitating to the human spirit.[7] Radical suffering includes the abuse of children, war, and assaults on other innocent people. I wish that such suffering were rare. It is not. The statistics are shocking in terms of the frequency of sexual and physical abuse of children. And abuses of women in wartime such as torture and rape are too numerous to count.

Catastrophic suffering is not a vehicle for growth. Rather, it is suffering which cries out for healing. Unfortunately, the victims of such abuse often struggle with self-hate, extraordinary shame and guilt. They need and deserve an unlimited outpouring of compassion and expression of rage from the Christian community. Women who thus suffer have an enormous challenge to embark on a spiritual journey of healing and growing awareness of the deep goodness within. Healing needs to include a gradual letting go of the notion that "there must be something wrong with me" because of what was done to me. The image and understanding of God as "companion-sufferer"[8] is essential. It is not hard to image the Jesus who called the little children to himself weeping as he did over Lazarus, for all the suffering innocents.

Saint Teresa of Avila writes that the compassion in God's eyes tells her that God is always there and that God kneels over the earth (us) like a Divine medic. God's love "thaws the holy in us."[9] When a sense of the holy is frozen through radical suffering, we are invited to open ourselves to the healing embrace of the "Divine Medic" made present through human beings who radiate compassion, encouragement and sacred presence. The beauty and endurance of nature has the power to offer hope and comfort in situations of intense suffering. It is a courageous choice for the radical sufferer to put her hand out to the Divine companion sufferer and walk the path of the Spirit toward healing and wholeness. Countless women who have struggled with this kind of suffering have put out their hands and walked this amazing path. Those who make this journey enrich the universe with their strength.

Often a woman who has experienced radical suffering survives by disassociating from her experience. She may come to a "place" in her mind which offers solace, and, perhaps, God's presence. That "place," that "corner of the room" is outside of herself. Because of that wise way of protecting herself, she learns anew that the Spirit of God lives in her and that within her very being Love, the Holy One, finds a worthy dwelling place. It is certainly a moment of Divine in-breaking when a radical sufferer recognizes herself as a place where Sacred Presence chooses to be. Prayer mantras for a woman who has known radical suffering might be these:

> Suffering Companion God, help me to rage against the suffering I have endured.
>
> Suffering Companion God, heal me and let me see radiance and beauty in my whole being.
>
> Suffering Companion God, I notice and welcome your gracious Spirit present in my healing self.

Considering radical suffering is an appropriate prelude to a consideration of global suffering. In a time of war, rape and killing are rampant. In places of extreme poverty, it is not uncommon to see women holding their dead children as Mary held the body of her son. In silent prayer, we hold these suffering sisters.

Global and Earth Suffering

Our personal struggles and sufferings often serve to heighten our awareness of other human beings and of all created things. No woman can better console a mother whose son is killed in war than the one who has also lost a son. There is a political song from Chile that says to love means not to hide your face.[10] Perhaps this desire to hide our faces is to protect ourselves from global suffering and the degradation of the earth. While it is sometimes appropriate to step back from faces of suffering, we must also allow ourselves to be summoned by a suffering face. Through contemplation of such a face, a stranger becomes a neighbor. The face of a woman in Darfur so very sad and vulnerable; of a young gay man tortured by hatred; of the wife and children left alone by the war death of their spouse and father are faces that beg for response. The faces of struggle around the globe and the face of our fragile, wounded earth can direct us to prayer and to action born of prayer. Contemplation of the outcomes of materialism, greed, egoism and violence can lead to a passion for mystical prayer and for justice in our world.

In conclusion, we pray that we are able to believe with Saint Paul that nothing can separate us from the love of God, no matter how tragic, powerful or difficult (see Romans 8:38–39). This is not an easy truth to embrace in the face of serious personal suffering or the widespread suffering across the globe and throughout all of creation. However, our faith offers us a path we could name "God with us" or "I have come that you might have life" (see John 10:10).

At the end of a chapter which includes very difficult dimensions of life, I want to bring forth the face of Etty Hillesum, a young woman who was imprisoned and eventually died at Auschwitz. She was called the thinking heart of the barracks and had an extraordinary relationship with God. Prior to her arrest, Etty reports that she became very attuned to the vulnerability of God. She wrote to God in her diary concerning the social situation of Jews in Amsterdam: "Alas, there doesn't seem very much you yourself can do about our circumstances, our lives...but we must help you to defend your dwelling place inside us to the last...."[11] Hillesum takes it upon herself to console God, a response worthy of contemplation. The hope in Etty Hillesum's mystic heart is, I believe, a source of hope for all of us, and that hope radiates from her words:

> All I want to say is this: the misery here is quite terrible, and yet, I often walk along with a spring in my step along the barbed wire. And then time and again it soars straight from my heart...the feeling that life is glorious and magnificent, and that one day we shall be building a whole new world.[12]

Indeed, nothing shall separate us from the love of God.

FOOD FOR THOUGHT

1. Each Good Friday in Chicago, a group of people gather to celebrate the traditional devotion of the Stations of the Cross in a contemporary way. The leaders choose significant global or national struggles, suffering and injustices and remember them with song and prayer. The group moves through the downtown area stopping at buildings that symbolize injustice to prisoners, racism and violence. What struggles would you name as the "stations" to remember this coming Good Friday?

2. Staying with the images of the Stations of the Cross, call to mind the three times Jesus met women along the way—his mother, Mary, the women of Jerusalem and a woman named Veronica who wiped his face. These women risked their safety and were courageous in order

to offer support to the man condemned to death. Reflect on a time in your life when you struggled to be courageous. Have you ever chosen to stand by someone others have rejected? Reflect on the times you have chosen to be present to someone who is seriously ill over a long period of time, or some similar experience.

3. In the Stations of the Cross, we are reminded that Jesus fell three times. Ponder times you have "fallen" because you carry heavy burdens, are impatient with yourself or feel like giving up in the face of your struggles. What assistance is available to you? How open are you to accepting help from family and friends?

4. One of the Stations describes Jesus being stripped of his clothes. Can you recall a time in your life when you were unfairly stripped of something that was yours—wages, reputation, health, possessions? As you struggle or remember struggling with these kinds of experiences, how did you manage?

RITUAL

1. Gather a candle, a small box with a lid, a pen, five or six small strips of paper and a dish with water in it. Arrange these items into a beautiful altar that represents struggle. Add any other meaningful symbols if you wish.

2. Light the candle and take some deep, quieting breaths. Then take your paper strips and pen in hand. Take your time to call to mind struggles or sufferings you face right now. These might be daily struggles, grief, radical suffering of your own or someone you know, midlife struggles or global concerns. Write a struggle on each piece of paper and place it in the box. Now, hold the box full of struggles in the palm of your hand and ponder these questions in silence:

    About which struggles in this box might I do something?

    Which struggles or sufferings need to be endured?

3. If you know a melody for these words, sing them, repeating it several times: "Our God hears the cries of the poor. Blessed be our God." If

you do not know a melody, simply pray these words. Open the box, take out each strip, and say aloud each struggle. Use the water to sprinkle the paper and the box with "living water"...the water of healing and compassion. Make the Sign of the Cross on yourself with this water.

4. Pray:

Dear God, may the gift of this box of struggles bring me closer to you, Sacred Presence, Companion Sufferer. Amen.

CHAPTER FIVE

• NURTURING •

*One of Julian's [of Norwich] most important messages is to live in
joy, to allow the Spirit's touch to create in us a deep and abiding
sense of holy pleasure and delight.*[1]

—Elizabeth A. Dreyer

Without nurturing, nothing grows—not plants, not polar bears, not
children of any color, not minds, not consciousness, not relationships
with God or any other being. Years ago I heard a striking example of
the need for nurturing. Infants less than six months old and without
parents due to war tragedies were being cared for in a hospital in a big
city. Their physical needs were being met, yet the babies were losing
vitality and actually going into psychic withdrawal. A therapist was
called in and put forth a remedy he said was urgent to save the lives of
the children. On each crib he ordered that a sign be taped that read:
"Every two hours this child must be lovingly held for fifteen minutes."
That was done, and the children were saved. Without nurturing, we are
not able to go on making our contribution to the universe or living in
joy at the Spirit's touch.

Very early in life an infant develops a sense of who he or she is
through relationships with others. Even when nursing, the little one is
content only when it senses its mother is comfortable. Both are engaged
in an emotional relationship that moves toward the greater well-being
of each. A sense of oneself as a person who attends to what is going on

in relationship is the basis of continuing psychological growth.[2] Girls' and women's ability to relate well to others has a great deal to do with their self-esteem. The desire to be in relationship is natural for women. This desire is not a sign of dependency; rather, relationship is one key hallmark of women's spirituality. Of course, this gift of relating can also cause trouble if we neglect our own needs. But I want to underline how relationships are at the heart of our spiritualities as we cocreate with the Spirit of God who each of us will become in this world.

Who among us does not want to gift the universe with the legacy of a life of compassion, courage and creativity through the ways we relate to God, neighbor, earth, self and all beings? These qualities, so needed in our world, don't simply bubble up in us on demand. They need to be carefully nurtured over a lifetime. We can do this nurturing through practice and prayer and peacemaking. You may have heard that the best way to live a life of compassion, courage and creativity is to do God's will. Once I was told that the best expression of God's will are the words of Scripture, "I came that you may have life, and have it abundantly" (see John 10:10). The Scripture quotation gives a broad sense of God's will. It is refreshing to imagine God wanting for us what is life-giving. Often, when faced with a serious choice or decision, people say, "I want to do God's will." What exactly does that mean? Some believe that everything that is supposed to happen in their lives is written down in the mind of God, and it is their task to access that information. Some believe that God's will is always the opposite of what they themselves want or will. Some envision God's will as ominous or oppressive, certainly as demanding and difficult. Have you heard someone say to relatives whose loved one died in a tragic way, "I'm sorry, but it was God's will"? These ways of seeing God's will are limited and imply a narrow and punishing God. While the phrase is commonly used, few can explain what it means to them.

Imagine what might be the will of a God named Love, Holy Presence, Wisdom, Caring Father or Mother? Life in abundance would include noticing and nurturing gifts, noticing and resisting what is harmful to ourselves and others. A God named Love would will compassion. A God named Holy Presence would will right relationship. A God named Wisdom or Sophia would will reverence for creation and inclusivity at our table. God, unfathomable Mystery, does not impose on us a detailed map of the path of our lives. God draws us toward embracing the good and letting go of what is death-dealing within us and around us. It is this call of the spirit to nurture abundant life that makes it essential to consider some ways to feed us in our quest for spiritual vitality.

A Story That Nurtures

Stories are a great source of nurturance and inspiration. This one may be familiar to you but I hope you hear it in a new key, inviting you to reflection and empowerment. The story may also help readers notice when what we do is enough; that through intentional living we are indeed "building the universe."

The story of the woman who anointed Jesus describes a courageous, compassionate and creative woman doing "what she could" (Mark 14:8).[3] In Mark's version of the story, the unnamed woman, who was a servant or entertainer, broke open an alabaster jar of very costly ointment of nard. She poured the nard on Jesus' head. The woman has no status and is criticized for using the precious ointment. The headline in the Bethany paper, if they had one, might read "Servant Woman Anoints Healer" or "Crazy Woman Wastes Precious Nard on Wandering Preacher." It would depend on your perspective, on how you see this drama.

The anointing was a lavishly loving act that took great courage and had to be Spirit-inspired. The woman was silent; she would have been sent away if she had spoken. She intuited that Jesus needed to be anointed and she acted without hesitation. She was determined to use the power within her to express compassion in this extravagant way. Jesus, the recipient of her sacred and generous act, told her critics that she had anointed him for his burial and that she had done what she had the power to do.

That line—she did what she had the power to do—would have been a comfort to her and can be a comfort to us. She did not have the power to stop the betrayal of Jesus or help him carry the cross or give him a drink, console his mother or pray with him in the garden of Gethsemane. The woman at this supper was incapable of traveling the way of the cross with Jesus and was not called to do so. This was her moment. Undoubtedly, she hesitated. No one had expectations of her. She could have done nothing. And yet some consideration of the person of Jesus and a sense of what was being asked of her moved her to act as she did. The reason I consider the fact that she did this one thing, though there were many things she could not do, is that we need to hear this. Countless women "do what they have the power to do" and also feel responsible to do a host of other kind and just things. It takes times of prayer and reflection, of being open to the spirit, to know what it is compassion asks of us, and that we acknowledge what we do not have the power to do. It is common for women to look at circumstances in our families—divorce, economic distress, alcoholism—or in the world—the war in Iraq, abuse of women in Darfur, poverty in India—and feel responsible to take action to fix things. This story makes clear that the woman did what was within her power, and Jesus acknowledged and celebrated that. It was enough. Mark reminds us that wherever the good news of Jesus' life is proclaimed in the world, what this woman has done "will be told in remembrance of her" (Mark 14:9).

This story nurtures us in a number of ways. Considering the low place of women in her culture and her status in the group gathered at Simon's house, it is not difficult to imagine how much courage it took for her to do what she did. Breaking the alabaster jar, pouring the nard on Jesus and touching him were risky. Moved with compassion, she did what she had the power to do. This nameless servant woman listened to the Spirit, paid attention to her intuition and did something to nurture a fellow human being in need.

Another important aspect of the story is Jesus' response. Since the woman could not speak and certainly could not defend herself, Jesus addressed the group gathered, appropriately thanking and memorializing the woman who poured the precious ointment of compassion over him. What a mutual experience this anointing turned out to be. What a moment of abundant life.

If you can, take some meditation time to read this story (see Mark 14:3–9), and allow it to bring to your mind times when you did something that took courage, compassion and creativity. Such actions happen more often than you imagine in very different circumstances than those of the anointing story, yet no less powerful. Many ways may come to mind in which you nurture fullness of life in people and also in yourself.

Spiritual Nurturing

An assumption with which I write is that each reader of this book, whatever her age, wants to become as fully spiritually alive as possible. I trust that we do intend to leave that legacy of a life of compassion, courage and creativity to the universe with the help of the Spirit of God. Whether you are just beginning to notice the spark of the divine in life, awakening to Sacred Presence, or are in a place of struggle or dryness, you are in a place where the Spirit dwells. Whether you cannot endure one moment of delayed gratification or the smallest affront to your ego, or you are pouring yourself out for others to the point of exhaustion and self-harm, you can still thirst for the sacred in life. It is incredibly energizing to be aware that you are invited to cocreate your life, yourself and your contribution to the universe in partnership with the Spirit of God. The place to begin is wherever you find yourself right now.

An important aspect of your response to that invitation is to find ways to nurture the relationship. But first, it is helpful to consider some characteristics of women's spirituality that we seem to hold in common and that imply the need for and role of nurturing, such as balance, connectedness with other women and appropriate self-love.

Nurturing Through Neighbor Love

Surely, our compassionate response to people in need is prompted by the Spirit, and neighbor love is among the strongest mandates in the Gospels. Understood in its fullest meaning, neighbor love in action has the power to transform the world. The women who mentor and inspire us incarnate the practice of loving their neighbors well—Catherine of Siena, Dorothy Day, Mother Teresa, Etty Hillesum, friends who have worked in the Peace Corps or with Doctors Without Borders, and so many more. We weep with the mothers of Americans who have lost children in the military, mothers of Iraq whose little ones have been killed before their eyes, mothers of Darfur whose babies have no food. And we reach out and act as the Spirit urges us and our life circumstances allow. In relation to these tragic realities of our time, we feel compassion, we send the loving energy of prayer and we do what we have the power to do. In the face of enormous concerns such as war and global poverty, we can feel powerless and paralyzed. It takes faith to acknowledge that noticing, lamenting, having compassion and doing what is possible in your local situation is enough. Similarly, the woman who anointed Jesus with nard did what might be regarded by some as small and by some as inappropriate; however, it was within the range of possibility for her. And it was enough. Catherine of Siena, a Dominican mystic and activist, has powerful words encouraging love of the world and its people, "I long to see you swallowed up—drowned—in the fire of God's blazing charity, stripped of your unfit clothing and completely covered, clothed in the fire of the Holy Spirit."[4]

It is safe to say that neighbor love is constitutive of women's spirituality, even when it is costly. Most of us aren't in Doctors Without Borders or in the streets of India, yet the intensity of the fire of the Spirit is needed every day as we parent, care for elderly parents, work sensitively with coworkers. The Spirit also empowers us to channel love to the four corners of the world. In a sermon given years ago, German theologian Hans Küng described Jesus' compassion: "He went about dumping mercy indiscriminately everywhere he walked." That is without question the Christian way in its fullness.

In my life experience, I have met countless women who are expert at loving their neighbors. However, they become exhausted and even burned out. Nurturing others is surely the Christian call, but balance is essential. When a person is "clothed in the fire of the Holy Spirit," a way to balance life is a challenge. There is a story in Mark's Gospel in which Jesus seems to struggle with the issue of balance (see Mark 6:45–51). He sends his disciples off in a boat, says goodbye to the crowds and goes off to the hills to pray. Clearly, he needs some time to contemplate and some time just to be alone. It's been a busy day, perhaps frustrating. In the midst of his prayer, he noticed that a wind had come up and the rowing was difficult. He leaves his hill, his much-needed time alone, to go and check on the disciples. Even then, "He intended to pass them by." That sentence says to me that he was intending to continue with his time by and for himself. However, the disciples whom he loved got scared, completely undone by the storm and seeing him on the water, and Jesus went to them. It is encouraging to see in Jesus the struggle for trying to balance what is psychologically and spiritually healthy for himself and what compassion and neighbor love ask in the moment. The saints wrestled with the same concern as have mothers, teachers, ministers, doctors and others trying to live spiritual lives. It's a judgment call as to when we "touch the face of God" responding to another, and when we go to that hill to tend to the needs of our own souls. The decisions aren't easy; life in the Spirit is complex, and guidance from within and from wise ones around us is helpful, if not essential. Victor Hugo wrote in *Les Miserables*, "To love another is to see the face of God." Neighbor love is the active dimension of the spiritual life. Contemplation is the source of the energy to love well.

Nurturing Through Contemplation

As you may recall from chapter one, contemplation—that "long, loving look at the real"—assists us in noticing what is within and all around us. Probably no one reading this book lives in a monastery where contemplative prayer is the center of daily life. And our culture certainly does not encourage us to use time to gaze lovingly at the real. But culture is a complex animal. Aspects of it also lead many people to long for the spiritual. This new consciousness is evident in the broad interest in Buddhist meditation, the large numbers traveling to spiritual conferences and the number of centering prayer groups springing up all around the country. Such involvements are a source of hope and physical, psychic and spiritual health. New and broad interest in prayer and spirituality among people who are extraordinarily busy, sometimes frustrated with their lives, indicates that Holy Presence is never really absent. The Spirit extends a strong invitation in any situation to notice the sacred. Sometimes we actually do.

Yes—the purpose of contemplative time is to move away from demanding activity for a while for the deeper purpose of regarding Sacred Presence and allowing that Presence to renew, refresh and transform us. Contemplation is an experience of opening our minds and hearts to the Spirit. Think about it, about what it means to open your heart. Remember the experience of an exquisite sunset whose beauty opened you up and filled you with awe. Remember seeing a baby born and being opened by the miracle which brought you to tears or to your knees, being filled with amazement. Remember when you threw the basketball and made the points that won the game for your team in the last seconds of play, and you were filled with a sense of accomplishment, excitement, joy. Remember tender words, perhaps life-changing, from the love of your life, igniting a flame in you that spread like a wildfire through your whole being. And in that moment, everything and everyone you saw had a loving place in your open heart. Those experiences opened you and filled you. As Christians, our baptism calls us to turn to the source of the amazement, the joy which awakens and fills us. Contemplation empowers us as we welcome into the home of our open hearts the Holy Spirit of who dwells within and all around us. The Spirit has gifts and fruits to offer us. Desire and prayer give us access to love, joy, peace, patience, kindness, generosity, faithfulness, gentleness and self-control (see Galatians 5:22–23). Without these gifts of the Spirit, there is no power to nurture the universe.

For those "out of the monastery" dwellers, creativity enables us to arrange contemplative time and space. Of course, if a quiet room, a big chair and a candle are available, we are in luck! But there are many other creative alternatives. Walking the dog, bike-riding, bird-watching and driving with the radio off open small windows into contemplative regard of the Divine Presence in the ordinary experiences of life. Slowly, but noticeably, our hearts expand to embrace the world in love.

Connectedness Among Women
In addition to the need for balancing the active and contemplative way of being in the world, women's spirits are nurtured by connectedness with other women. Developing a kinship with nature and neighbor also creates a non-hierarchical model of relationship. A circular, mutual, collaborative way of relating which is intentional in women's friendships and various groupings is vital. This non-hierarchical way of relating is an alternative to the way that is dominant in the culture. Circles of women who embrace and are empowered to relate in this manner compatible with the Spirit's fruits—peaceful, kind, self-controlled, generous and joyful—are changing themselves and the world. Like a pebble in a pond, they send out circular rings of influence. They are a holy undercurrent of an alternative way of relating. It is clear that women's circles are forming throughout the world for the purpose of support, shared wisdom and good times. The crises of our time and evolution of our culture require that we see these circles as existing also with the intention of birthing a new way of being in the world. Our intention for change from "the way things are" to a non-hierarchical and Spirit-inspired way of relating needs to be explicit and cause for celebration.

Women friends are treasures. They are a safe haven, a place for sharing, healing and fun. Women gather to study, to laugh, to pray and to play. Such solidarity often leads to greater health, life and passion for those who suffer. We can be bread of life for one another.

In 2006, three women—a Muslim, a Christian and a Jew—came together to write a children's book about God. They found that they could not write that book until they learned thoroughly what faith meant to each of them. Their experience of honest talk, mutuality and love was transformative and productive. While they postponed the children's book, together they wrote *The Faith Club*. The book documents their experience of a challenging and bonding journey toward understanding. The women and their work exemplify a mutual, collaborative circle—a community of equals that nurtures and enriches. Their book offers a methodology for starting a faith club. In the good company of one another, they created a way to birth a book through dialogic interaction. One author's words summarize this experience well: "I still get spiritual nourishment and stimulation from my Faith Club soul mates as we continue to meet to discuss religion in the world and in our own messy lives."[5] The courageous adventure these women experienced energizes our souls and invites us to imagine how we might make choices that offer spiritual nourishment. Spiritual nourishment and stimulation and a relationship of soul mates—a rather rich reward for their courageous adventure in faith.

The faith club group had a common spiritual quest as their reason for coming together. Some of our friendships and circles to which we belong have an explicit spiritual dimension, others not. Because the Spirit hovers absolutely everywhere, no gathering is free of her influence. There are certain relationships that are particularly precious because encounters with those women affect us at the soul level. Individual women friends committed to each other can pray together, share suffering and disappointments and even notice when we aren't being honest with ourselves, God or one another. What a gift such a friend is! The face of God is present in her e-mail, in her gentle call to acknowledge something, in the flowers she sends on the one-month anniversary of your mother's death. In circles of women gathered with a spiritual intention, challenges as well as energizing experiences are inevitable. We bring our whole self to the circle—our weaknesses and strengths, our negative and positive dimensions. Someone's growing edge can be a threat to another member. While one woman's good fortune evokes delight from most circle members, from one, envy spills out right into the center of the circle. On the other hand, the vulnerability, depth of honesty, attentiveness to the needs of one another and the Spirit present in one another makes the circle deserving of the name "friends of God" and the relationship among the women is that of soul sisters.

Appropriate Self-Love

In addition to the balancing of neighbor love and contemplative space and the enriching experience of connecting with women friends and colleagues, the particular way we nurture and care for ourselves is a mark of women's spirituality. For many women, healthy self-love is elusive. It is difficult for some to distinguish appropriate self-care from selfishness. We tend to judge ourselves as being our best when we pour ourselves out to the point of exhaustion and don't count the cost. The notion of "earning" God's love and that of family, friends and even employers has often been tied to never putting yourself first or taking time to do what you want to do. The message of self-denial and sacrifice has been so loud and often repeated in our religious history that we may have spent very little time on how to love ourselves appropriately. What, exactly, is appropriate? Certainly, it is not the burn-out, make-of-yourself-a-servant route. On the other hand, neither is spiritually healthy self-care the narcissistic, indulgent focus on our own wants promoted by affluent culture. We need to discern what Jesus' central message to love our neighbor as ourselves (see Mark 12:31) means in twenty-first century Christian spirituality. Our spirituality is characterized by a deep and inclusive love. It stretches us to regard our children, students, friends and enemies as another self to love. And the way we are able to love ourselves affects the quality of relationship we have with all the "neighbors" we encounter. Pray with these questions, keeping in your mind and heart how you might bring the Spirit's gifts of joy, patience, peace and kindness to the world through loving yourself well:

- What enables me to open myself to the Spirit?
- What little or great things sustain me so that I can endure, savor and celebrate my life while contributing to the universe?
- Am I able to pour the precious ointment of compassion on my life and know that what I do is enough?

While others did so, Jesus offered no objections to the use of nard in the anointing story (see Mark 14:4–6). Your nard may be time, nature, friends, laughter, a hot bath, a soul-food meal. Don't allow the critical voices within you to tell you not to waste the precious nard on yourself. Hear God telling you to attend to yourself with reverence and care, so you will learn how to attend to your neighbor. This realization might be among the more difficult aspects of your prayerful activity, your life in the Spirit. It takes courage, compassion and creativity to find ways to express your love of self as well as you love your neighbor and your world.

To conclude this chapter, I want to put before you two ways of opening yourself to the Spirit. There are many ways, but these are available to everyone. Creation, in all its mind-boggling wonder, inspired the mystics, was central in Jesus' teaching and invites us to see with new eyes.

Sources of Nurturing

All creation has come into being through what is poorly named the "Big Bang" or the great flaring forth that took place 13.7 billion years ago. Since all life is part of that event, all life is connected at the most basic level. Since then, an ongoing act of creation called *cosmogenesis* has been in process. For believers, God is at the heart of this great evolutionary movement. This process is, quite literally, the greatest source of nurturance there is.

If beauty and wonder nurture the human spirit, then the universe is bursting with nurturing possibilities. Though human beings have always revered the sun, moon and stars, scientists now provide detailed information that was unavailable even one hundred years ago. We have existed a mere twenty years or so with the Hubble telescope as our companion. The remarkable pictures of the planets and space can now become an integral part of our spiritual lives. At this moment, the universe invites us to nurture a new perspective, allowing ourselves to be transformed by this new vision. We are at a crossroads in the evolutionary process which challenges us to see ourselves in relation to creation in a new way. Humans need to become more universe-conscious. We need to see the sun, all creatures and earth with new eyes. Let me just suggest what this might mean. To be a universe-conscious human being is to be one who is connected in mind and heart with the whole of life.

Consider the sun which converts four million tons of mass energy to light each second. It will never recapture that energy, a gift by which we live. Photosynthesis is the Earth's way of receiving the sun's gift. This solar giving has been compared with the care loving parents offer their children.[6] Hafiz, a beloved Persian poet of the fourteenth century, speaks of the sun's generosity:

> Even
> After
> All this time
> The sun never says to the earth,
> "You owe
> me."
> Look
> What happens

With a love like that,
It lights the
whole
Sky.[7]

While sunrises and sunsets are enjoyed and admired, deeper awareness of the sun's gifting evokes a deep sense of interconnectedness.

We humans are rightly accused of being anthropocentric—stuck on ourselves at the expense of other species. It is well to remember that while humans may have pride of place when it comes to ethical demands, we are also called to respond to our neighbor the whale, the dolphin and the rainforest. The poet Brian Patrick reminds us that we must love all our neighbors as ourselves.[8] We cannot say to anything in creation, "I have no need of you." Everything is sacred.[9]

Our earth is threatened. To put our ears against the body of the earth and hear the pleas of her rivers, her forests, her plants and birds and beasts is to enter into a love affair with God. The universe is filled in all its dimensions with the energy of the Spirit. What a spellbinding source of nurturance and amazement!

The heavens are telling the glory of God;
and the firmament proclaims his handiwork. (Psalm 19:1)

A Practice that Nurtures

For those who are able, walking with open eyes, heart and mind is a simple, accessible spiritual practice. There is a difference between simply walking, and a walking meditation. When we simply take a walk, it can't be assumed that we are involved with creation. It's possible to be concerned with plans, speed or figuring out some problem. What makes walking meditation different is that you dwell in the present moment and walk mindfully.

The Buddha was once asked, "What do you and your disciples practice?" And Buddha replied, "We sit, we walk and we eat." The questioner said, "Everyone sits, walks and eats." The Buddha told him,

"When we sit, we know we are sitting. When we walk, we know we are walking. When we eat, we know we are eating."[10] The kind of walking in which we *know* we are walking is the walking that is prayer, communing with what the environment offers.

Thich Nhat Hahn, a Vietnamese Buddhist monk known for his wisdom about meditation, insists that walking meditation nourishes the body and the spirit. His familiarity with this practice moves him to entreat us to kiss the earth, massage the earth with our feet in our walk. He insists that our mother, the earth, will heal us and we will heal her.[11] Often, the peace and joy the earth has to give enters the person walking, resulting in wonder and a heart full of praise. Wherever you are, such walking is possible; your feet can connect with earth on a city street, in a park, in a beautiful garden, on the shore of the ocean or a lake. Walk gently on our mother earth and she will nurture you.

We live in the sun's radiance. I imagine that Jesus was conscious of this when he called us to be light. "You are the light of the world" (Matthew 5:14). This chapter has been about how to avoid hiding our light under a bushel by failing to find ways to nurture the Divine spark that dwells in each of us. The woman who anointed Jesus did not hide her light. The sun pours out its light generously. The Spirit is present always and everywhere. Choosing to give and receive nurture as we walk the spiritual path is the invitation of this chapter. "Do what you have the power to do," enriching the universe through your compassion, courage and creativity. The evolving universe awaits our light; our responsibility is to embrace the sustaining gift that enkindles the fire of the Spirit in us.

FOOD FOR THOUGHT

1. Create in your imagination a circle of three or four women who have nurtured your body, mind and spirit. Recall experiences of family, mentors in school, good friends and elders. Name the ways in which each has gifted you, nurtured you. How has each contributed to who you have become in your life?

2. Consider what you find beautiful and awesome in the universe. Name and appreciate those elements that nurture you—favorite flowers, the full moon, a particular lake. Is there one creation experience that shaped you? Write or draw aspects of that experience.

3. How you do practice appropriate self-love? What thoughts do you think, and what actions do you take to nurture your love of yourself?

4. Recall an event when you acted with courage, even though you were afraid. Savor that event and give thanks.

RITUAL

1. Arrange a space with a candle and several pairs of your shoes. If this ritual is done in a group, each person can bring a pair of shoes. Light the candle. Recall places you have walked in these shoes that have nurtured you.

   - *Did you hike in the woods?*
   - *Did you walk with a child?*
   - *Did you place your foot on the earth, aware that it was holy ground?*
   - *Was your walk a source of beauty, of relationship?*
   - *Did it take you to a place in which you needed courage?*
   - *How has where you have walked brought you to the place where you "do what you have the power to do"?*
   - *Can you recall the details of a slow, meditative walk?*

2. Take a slow meditative walk. Be conscious of the earth as holy ground, and pick up some things along the way that help you touch the face of the God.

3. Closing Prayer:

   The world has many paths. Come, Holy Spirit, help me to walk the paths of compassion, courage and creativity. I long to be nurtured by my many walks in life, that I may do what I have the power to do as the woman who anointed Jesus did. I also ask for the grace and strength to walk a mile in other people's shoes in order to understand and to love. Amen.

CHAPTER SIX

• TRANSFORMING •

To embrace a God of mystery means that we live open to surprise, ready to respond in radically new ways to the One who never ceases to amaze. Embracing a God of mystery means that we live in relative comfort with the unknown, grounded in the assurance that the divine is ever present, ever at work in wondrously creative ways.[1]

—Judy Cannato

Transforming—an odd title, you may say. And what does transforming have to do with prayer? You are right this moment in the process of transforming yourself and of being transformed and so is this society, culture, planet and universe. This chapter is an invitation to say yes to a life journey in which you actively engage with the Spirit of God to become your most authentic, free, deep and beautiful self possible. Prayer is a vital part of this kind of journey. In silence, with words, alone or with family, friends or community, praying helps make the journey possible. Prayer helps you notice the call of the Spirit, strengthens you when you face suffering or disappointment, offers a way to express thanks for breakthroughs and praise for miracles along the way.

Did you know that every seven years you have all new skin? You are experiencing a "makeover" and yet you are yourself. Did you know that at age twenty-eight you reach your physical peak and that from then on—very gradually—your body moves away from its peak state? You are experiencing a transformation and yet you are yourself. American culture emphasizes physical transformation as a major industry. In the corner of my computer screen, there is an ad for some lotion in which the face of a woman goes through forty years of increasing wrinkles in the course of five or six seconds. Thank God, Mother Nature is more gentle with us. And so is God. At age twenty-eight, many of us are just getting a sense of the spiritual life, and the journey goes on for a lifetime of transforming activity. We are all on an inner and outer journey, on a personal and global journey. It can be the adventure of our lifetime or mere existence and drudgery. Saying yes to this spiritual journey puts each of us on a path which transforms ourselves and the universe. Because this journey doesn't have an arrival point, the journey itself is home.

Not any person still living and breathing is in a finished or completed state, nor is the world in which we live. We inhabit an incomplete universe on the move. Imagine yourself as a mini-universe aware that all that happens in the great universe is going on in you. The wondrous, sometimes disconcerting, realities of creation, struggle, birth, joy, color, destruction, grief, growth, delight and death are before us and within us. Transformation is about the movement and change needed for growth and spiritual development. It is easy to observe the change from a tiny seed to a blooming flower or the growth in a tiny baby to an energetic toddler. Noticing internal changes in our adult selves is more difficult. One way to get an idea of change in our own lives is to ask ourselves, "What was going on five or ten years ago in me in terms of views, attitudes, how I prayed, how I cared or not about myself, my friends, my world?" The change itself is likely to be evident. Whether or not the change is transformative is something to discern. Be prepared for remarkable discoveries.

It is the intent of God to heal the broken world, and God's intent is not in vain. The Spirit is constantly renewing, recreating and healing whatever is wounded in us and in the world. It is this creative work that supports the scriptural phrase, "I am making all things new" (Revelation 21:5). Sometimes it's very hard to believe that the Spirit is at work, that God is indeed making all things new. At the global level, we see wars, greed, abuse. Within ourselves we notice struggle, perhaps with addiction or hypocrisy or doing things to make a good impression. On the other hand, there are the pictures from the Hubble telescope, the man who single-handedly built schools for girls in Pakistan, the woman who established a clinic in a poverty-stricken village in Africa. Though the picture of global and personal life can at times be dismal, there is reason for hope because the transformative work of God will not be stopped.

Seeing Anew and Taking Action

Nurturing transforming activity requires seeing anew and intention. If we see ourselves and our neighbors as pregnant with wholeness and holiness, life holds great possibilities. What does it take to see the ground on which we walk as holy ground? Can you see the most ordinary moments of your life as sacred? Since it is God who does the transforming, how do you open your life to Holy Presence? What you are able to see determines how you can cocreate with God a path that can be called a spiritual journey. Seeing ourselves as in process and our God as loving and merciful is an amazing opening to transforming grace.

> I talked recently with a woman struggling to discern God's will for her life.
> "What do you most love to do?" I asked her.
> "I love to do things with my hands," she answered quickly. "I love to paint, to sew, to garden."
> "What longing underlies that love?" I asked.
> This took more thought and her answer came more slowly. "I really want to feel that I am making something beautiful, and that I have become part of that beauty."

"What longing lies beneath that?" I probed. "Try to feel, to sense that longing at your deepest core."

She closed her eyes, and there was a long silence. Then she answered softly: "I want to be part of God while God creates. My whole body, my whole self wants to be part of that power, part of that mighty river. It feels very fierce, very joyous."

She opened her eyes. "Is this really what God wants for me, too? I've always been a bit ashamed that what I really liked to do was material and physical. I never thought that was spiritual enough. Perhaps my hands knew it before I did—that God made me to be a creator in my own way. Maybe I'll begin to see other ways, too, in which I can create."[2]

What a discovery this woman made. She found transforming grace in herself and allowed it to impact her journey. A breakthrough!

To intend to do good, not evil; to be peaceful, not violent; to love and not hate sets the stage for transformation. A firm intention aligns us with the labor of God in God's birthing of love and justice. God does this birthing repeatedly; we can participate and be changed in the process. People sometimes mock intention—the way to hell is paved with good ones; however, it makes all the difference in the world. Intention indicates a conscious choice to give it my best shot—on this day or in this hour at work, with my child, in a difficult relationship.

Intention makes us conscious of a direction we choose to take. Giving voice to concrete intention is a way to make ourselves conscious that, with God's companionship, we can transform ordinary activities into sacred moments:

- I intend to live this day aware of God's presence within and around me.
- I intend to connect with the joys and sorrows in my life and the world, holding them with outstretched hands to our Compassionate God.

- I intend to make healthy choices for my body, mind and spirit today.
- I intend to look for the Divine spark in every human face I see today.
- I intend to notice beauty in some piece of nature today.
- I intend to hold, with God's strength and love, the wounded world in my heart.

Making even a few of these intentions puts before us possibilities for a day in the journey that holds promise. Which of the intentions connect with what is possible for you today? Sometimes it isn't possible to intend or commit ourselves to anything broader than what is immediately before us—an illness, a demanding encounter, a full work day. It is a time for self-compassion and for accepting *what is* in your life. On the other hand, the big picture pleads for our attention, our concern, our prayer and our action. It is a major challenge of a transforming journey in the Spirit to avoid guilt over being completely involved in our personal lives and to avoid paralysis in the face of the need for global transformation. Just to be aware of these possibilities helps, and prayer is a place in which all the universe can be included. You can experience compassion, hold in the prayer space of your heart and send loving energy to the four corners of the world in very little time and with very few words. Yet, you are conscious of world concerns and of your connectedness with all members of the human family. We've heard the expression, "Think globally, act locally." This phrase applies to a way of being grounded and reaching out, of being limited to one place and embracing any spot on the globe. Developing this perspective has transforming power and contributes to inner peace.

Transforming Grace, Alive and Well

The Dalai Lama says that peace will come to the world one heart at a time. This statement links personal and global transformation. It is a source of hope to realize that when we open ourselves individually to transforming grace, which is the activity of the Holy Spirit in our lives, we are affecting the world. Prayer and spiritual work is personal but never private. Loving, healing energy will not be contained in a small space. Imagine, instead, your own transforming perspective and intention making a notable difference in the world—one heart at a time. It is crucial to know that transformative changes in our own hearts and behaviors are key in bringing about "a new creation" (see Revelation 21:1) worldwide. Our species as well as each of us is on a spiritual journey and needs all the help it can get. We live in a time when women are becoming more influential as a transforming force and power for the survival of the vulnerable. Conscious of such disturbing realities as the trafficking of women, young boys and children as the world's number one crime in recent years, the sexual abuse of women on public buses in certain countries, the hunger of one-third of the children of the world and so many more travesties, we pray, we hope, we send loving energy into the universe. We are a part of the transformation.

Sometimes those who have effected personal and global transformation in a visible way draw us with magnetic force toward the process itself. Wangari Maathai exemplifies the connection between personal and global transformation. Her magnanimous spirit inspires us with a passion for change, growth and justice. In December 2004, Wangari became the first African woman to receive the Nobel Peace Prize. She was honored for her conviction that peace depends on our ability to sustain the earth.

Wangari Maathai founded the Green Belt movement in Nairobi. Through this movement, poor African women planted thirty million trees, work they continue to this day. The planting was a call for a peaceful transition to democracy. Other transformations accompanied the planting. The trees provide fuel, food, shelter and self-respect for the women and their families. Planting these trees provides symbols for the struggle for democracy and for peaceful resolution of conflict.[3] Women working together brought about change one tree at a time. The entire movement witnesses to the way women can seed and birth courage and hope in one another, transform the earth and call for peace. This project embodies elements of transforming grace which affect the personal, political and spiritual lives of the people of Nairobi. These women committed "labor" to their cause, and its fruit is magnificent and memorable. An inspiration for the courage to embrace the process of transformation in our own lives, Wangari Maathai spoke these words when she was awarded the Nobel Prize:

> In the course of history, there comes a time when humanity is called to shift to a new level of consciousness, to reach a higher moral ground. A time when we have to shed our fear and give hope to each other. That time is now.[4]

Does this true story awaken passion in you to desire transformation in yourself and the world? Do you experience the power of these women as an invitation? Or are you thinking that this woman was unusual and that you could never be as creative and courageous as she was or these women are? Wangari Maathai is sixty-plus years old. Sometime in the midst of her life, she discovered the spark of the spirit in herself; she let go of fears; she nurtured courage in herself and cocreated a path which transformed herself and her community. The women of Nairobi serve well as an inspiration for all women. Almost all of us intuit that we are on the edge of a crucial moment in the history of the human story on planet earth. As we stand here with this awareness, we may be afraid to take a step, yet we must. With the impetus of the Spirit, we can choose what is life-giving and resist what is death-dealing.

The voice within, summoning us to love good and avoid evil, is universal and calls us to the sacred task of transformation. For each of us, whether we've been on a spiritual journey for a long time or are just considering whether to see life that way, the time is now "to shed our fear and give hope to each other," as Wangari Maathai said.

It's possible to hear God speaking through this African woman or to sense the Spirit within calling us to a deeper spiritual life. Yet we hesitate. Do we see our lives as too ordinary or our hearts too stony? Ordinary means what—raising the next generation, bringing human values to the banking system, making a home permeated by love, teaching children their worth, practicing medicine with compassion or selling goods with a respect for customers. These "ordinary" life paths can call a new world into being. There's a promise in Scripture that can help us soften our stony hearts: "I will remove from your body the heart of stone and give you a heart of flesh" (Ezekiel 36:26). And still, some have great reluctance. Neither this Scripture quotation from long ago nor the example of the African women today move some of us to believe that personal and societal transformation are possible. Thinking that we ourselves or our world cannot be changed is paralyzing and breeds apathy. If we are tempted to think this way, it's time for a leap of faith, a prayer that cries out for courage, a burst of transforming fire. Often, some tragic or beautiful human event is the hand of God on our hearts of stone, breaking them open to allow sacred change.

We Don't Always Do What We Want

What is behind our inability to trust that "hearts of stone" can be changed to "hearts of flesh"? We have missed the mark. We are wounded and broken. We recognize ourselves in the words of Saint Paul, "For I do not do the good I want, but the evil I do not want is what I do" (Romans 7:19). If we are honest, we acknowledge things in us that are "not the good I want." We harbor desire for power and control over others and the earth. We nurture violence and lack compassion. We cling to disorder and skewed desire. Society is replete with powerful invitations to be completely self-focused, to see greed as a path to success or to measure one's worth by the number and quality of one's possessions. The mystery of evil is concretized in twenty-first century slavery, trafficking of people, genocide, self-hate, war and devastation of the planet. Each day we witness and help paint this harsh picture of right relationships gone awry. We witness serious brokenness. In the face of this wounded world and a wounded life, God is available as a source of relational, healing energy. It is very human to feel unable to open ourselves to healing grace because of fears. We can be afraid of not being worthy or that God would ask too much of us. We can be afraid of the chaos of life or that we are responsible for changing the world. In the face of fear, prayer and stories of women on this journey are sources of courage. Dawna Markova's is a powerful, hopeful, transforming prayer.

> I will not die an unlived life,
> I will not go in fear
> Of falling or catching fire,
> I choose to inhabit my days,
> To allow my living to open to me,
> To make me less afraid,
> More accessible,
> To loosen my heart
> Until it becomes a wing,
> A torch, a promise.
> I chose to risk my significance:
> To live.
> So that which comes to me as seed,
> Goes to the next as blossom,
> And that which comes to me as blossom,
> Goes on as fruit.[5]

Who do you know who has lived this prayer from seed to blossom to fruit?

The Transformative Way

Each of us can pray for, and expect to notice, the tremendous woundedness in the world; experience a broken heart in the face of such suffering; and allow this suffering to awaken in us a desire for change.

Since the journey will be difficult, we know we can't walk this path alone. Sensing this truth is a sign of readiness for the transformational journey. It signals that "your salvation is at hand." God's longing for you and your thirst for God converge, and you are gifted with the courage to take steps on the spiritual path that you and God will cocreate. The call isn't always as clear as what I have just described. However, even a more subtle conscious movement toward desire for spiritual transformation is a time for deep prayer:

> I open myself to healing grace.
> I ask for freedom from fear.
> I long for your loving energy, my God, to fill my whole being.
> Help me to believe that nothing can separate me from you.
> Give me the grace, please, to look beyond my own needs and wants.
> O Sacred Presence, show me the way.

Choose or create the mantra that expresses most clearly what you want to say to God at this moment in your spiritual life.

The mantra, "Show me the way," leads to reflection on the spiritual journey of Jesus and the wisdom and assistance available in his life and stories. Though Jesus knew the Jewish law and the prophets well, his confidence, authority and belief that he could make a difference were rooted in his Abba experience. This encounter with loving Divine Presence and the relationship with Abba that followed provided the foundation for his spiritual life. The path he created by walking it was inspired step-by-step through relationship with the Spirit. Important insight into the spiritual journey of Jesus is found in the scriptural account of his baptism and of his mission.

His baptism is described as an experience in which the Spirit descended on him and a voice called him "my son, the beloved" and said, "With you I am well pleased." Such affirmation from the God of his prayer, source of loving energy, gave Jesus courage for his adult spiritual journey in faith. Following his baptism, Jesus was led by the Spirit to the wilderness or desert and was tempted. This Gospel passage indicates that hard times, the desert, temptation, difficult experiences are not foreign to the spiritual journey; rather, they are to be expected (see Mark 1:10–13). Another moment recorded in the Gospels that demonstrates a key dimension of Jesus' spirituality is the account of his mission. He found the words for his mission in the writings of the prophet Isaiah, who may have been a mentor for Jesus. Those words announced that Jesus was filled or anointed with the Spirit of God for the purpose of bringing good news to the poor, releasing captives, giving sight to the blind and letting the oppressed go free (see Luke 4:16–18).

These two events, Jesus' baptism and statement of his mission, were the foundation of his spiritual life. He recognized the Spirit of God as the ever-present source and resource of his relational energy. After his contemplative experience and his struggle in the desert, he knew that the fire he felt, the energy available from the Spirit, was not for him alone. That energy led to preaching hope, liberating the enslaved, healing the blind and deaf and showing a way to those who had no way or were lost. He saw the need for the "long, loving look" of contemplation throughout his life. Jesus went forth from that contemplative place to birth love over and over again in the lives of people. Ahead of his time, he was often rejected as he responded to the call to mysticism, the call to inclusivity, the call to be a healing presence and to live with integrity, whatever that might cost. To choose a Christian spiritual path is to choose the way and the values Jesus put before the world, and to do so with a twenty-first century understanding of the world and the call.

Hope and joy well up in us when we see the mission of Jesus in modern dress continuing to emerge in activities, organizations and individual people. One inspiration is Habitat for Humanity and the thousands of people who carry out the mission of providing shelter, one house at a time; Greg Mortenson and his group that invest in education for girls in Pakistan and Afghanistan, one school at a time;

Mothers Against Drunk Driving, many of whom have lost a child in an accident, educating the world about the dangers of driving drunk one meeting, one activity at a time. We also see the little children leading us. A young boy heard about the lack of clean water in parts of Africa; he began to collect money. He traveled to Africa and financed projects to assure clean water, one village at a time. Mattie Stepanek died in June 2004 at age thirteen, but not before leaving us five books of poetry. He identified himself as a peacemaker. His way of nonviolence continues to inspire the nation.

In addition to organizations committed to missions transforming our world and children leading the way, there are the women. Bless the women with hearts of flesh and determination to transform the world in which they live and, of course, themselves. Some are rather well-known and some live down the street from any one of us. I am aware of countless women who live the mission of Jesus in hidden ways. There are those who meditate, contemplate and are mystics in the modern world. A grandmother taking to her prayer the need not to criticize her children's way of raising their daughter and changing her behavior and her relationships; a woman in her forties who works with mentally ill teenage boys convicted of crimes, who entreats God that "her boys" might have hope; a doctor in her thirties who meditates daily and who observes carefully how compassionate she is (or is not) with patients she encounters—these are among countless women who are in prayer and on mission. The call to live with integrity at any cost arises daily in their hearts and minds.

In stories and parables Jesus described what a spiritual journey entails. The famous Prodigal Son story has inspired artists and confounded the righteous (see Luke 15:11–32). Who doesn't know or hasn't been a prodigal? Today, prodigal behavior might be done with a credit card or an attitude of vindictiveness or blatant neglect where attentiveness is crucial. Isn't there at least a shadow of a prodigal in us all? In this story, we can easily understand the return of the desperate son. The father's running toward his son, a most uncommon behavior for Jewish fathers of this time, his compassionate embrace and the call for a welcome home party would startle readers of that time. What the father did may surprise us as well. How could Jesus give a clearer example of the extravagance of God's love for us? In the story of the lost sheep (see Luke 15:3–7), we see a consoling dimension of the Christian spiritual path—the tender longing of God for the lost. The rich young man (see Matthew 19:16–22) who had many possessions went away grieving when Jesus invited him to sell what he had and follow Jesus. This rich young man wasn't ready to sell and to follow. He was ready to grieve that he couldn't do it. Jesus and the Spirit invite and respect us. We can count on this as we walk the path. Whatever we are ready and willing to do at a given time is acceptable to God—simply wanting to want is a start.

In the kingdom parables of the treasure in the field (see Matthew 13:44) and the pearl of great price (see Matthew 13:45), the followers make a choice to pursue what is precious and to let go of anything that stands in the way of that pursuit. These few stories offer thoughts about the Christian way to ponder in meditative prayer:

> How does the lavish compassion of the father in the Prodigal Son story make me feel? How does it connect with any relationship in my own life?
>
> What is it that I cling to as the rich young man does? How do I grieve about that clinging?
>
> What is it that I regard as a pearl of great price? What would it cost me to pursue that?

You might wonder about how a first-century Palestinian Jew can offer spiritual wisdom to twenty-first century women living in the culture of the United States of America. The maleness of Jesus is an obstacle for some women, particularly at certain stages in their spiritual journey. However, the harmful patriarchal domination rejected by women is not found in the Jesus of the Gospels. Jesus' experience of the Divine was inclusive—his values, his commitment to changing the world remain relevant. The integrity with which he walked his spiritual path and his way of relating to all of creation are timeless. Jesus was open to transforming grace and participated in the creative and transforming work of the Spirit in the world as he was called to do. The allure of his life throughout the centuries confirms the authenticity of the path he cocreated with the Spirit of God. It is a great challenge and yet a possible way of life.

A chapter on transformation would not be complete without mentioning the challenge that spiritual writers name "the dark night of the soul." As Gerald May says in his book about the dark night, "...it is much more significant than simple misfortune."[6] It is a deep means of transformation, a movement toward indescribable freedom and joy.[7] While a "simple misfortune" can lead to the dark night, it is not the misfortune or the suffering which constitutes the "night." As the name signals, the dark night is a time when a person of faith feels she cannot see clearly; she has lost her way. Diane, who was mentioned earlier in the book, was confused, lost, felt abandoned by God when she received her cancer diagnosis. This was clearly a "dark night" and it was definitely a time of transforming grace. Her response to the significant tragic illness eventually brought her to freedom and to peace. It is the response of the human spirit of the one suffering that makes the difference in how the experience changes a person.

I recently read a story in which a young woman dying of AIDS expressed her terror and resistance to such suffering. Only later does she describe her illness as a great gift. This story is one way to understand the dark night experience as a journey from hating illness to calling it a great gift. Something happened in the depths of her soul—struggle, praying in and through her anger and grief, opening herself to Sacred Presence, accepting vulnerability. The freedom and joy Gerald May names are evident in the woman's new way of seeing. She describes every moment as precious to her, all the people in her life as treasures and her whole life as full of meaning. Claiming the dark night as a place of transformation and growth gives darkness its rightful place in the spiritual life. Darkness is a place where life and growth occur. A mother's womb is a dark place and in that place a fertilized egg becomes a human baby. The ground is dark and it is the place in which a planted seed bursts open and becomes a flower, tree or vine. The night sky at its darkest is the place where the beauty of stars and moon are visible. Seeing darkness as a place where life and beauty flourish helps prepare us to understand the role of the dark night in the spiritual life. The dark night can be a place of change and growth. Our immediate response to something that plunges us into some kind of physical, psychological or spiritual difficulty is to recoil from it. We deny it, despair over it, run from it. That is understandable; but we hope that, with the help of God, friends and our own inner strength and wisdom, we can enter this place and find life. Morrie, the man dying of Lou Gehrig's disease in the book *Tuesdays with Morrie*, allowed himself fifteen minutes of self-pity in the morning. After that, he got on with his day, and he not only found peace and life, he also inspired thousands through his story. It is a strengthening practice on this transforming journey to open ourselves to be inspired by people we know about and know in person who have grown in the darkness. To be inspired can be a prayer. It is the act of breathing in the spirit, courage and strength of powerful, ordinary people. They, and so many of our own family, friends and neighbors, encourage us as we make this journey which is actually our home.

The Journey Is Home

As this chapter concludes, I imagine some of you saying, "I'm worried about how I can get through tomorrow. This transformation business sounds like a bit of a leap." Believe me, "getting through tomorrow" is exactly what spiritual transformation is about. However, it adds a spark to that tomorrow. This spark is my awareness of God's presence and my choice to relate God to the world and the world to God. God may be saying, "Get busy, transform yourself and the world." But God is also always saying "I esteem and love you. I have profound respect for who you are, what you need and what you can bear." It is not such a radical leap to choose to be sensitive to the Spirit of the living God within you. In each chapter in this book, an experience present in ordinary life is described as a context from which we pray. Noticing, awakening, thirsting for God, struggling, nurturing are experiences through which transformation happens. Sometimes we are acutely aware of transformational change; at other times it is almost unconscious. The work of God is never at a standstill.

As we become more aware of ourselves as beings in a transformative process, it is clear that the process is both active and passive. Sometimes we are making choices for change in which we *do* a great deal; at other times we allow life events and God's grace to transform us. The capacity in us to be receptive is a tremendous asset in the spiritual life. Openness and responsiveness to the action of the Spirit make us like vessels ready to be filled with "living water" (John 4:10).

There is a mutual interaction between the path we travel and the way we pray. The path of transformation is rather like a spiral. We move in and out of different ways of praying. The image of a spiral (rather than the more traditional "ladder") more adequately describes the way we move forward—in a relationship, a practice, a behavior—and later find ourselves circling back to a former way of acting. This isn't a cause for worry; it is life. The nature of our prayer changes as we journey in faith. At times we speak and plead with God. In other moments, we are more reflective, move within ourselves and discover who we are and the Spirit's presence within. In a dark night experience, prayer itself can be a great struggle. There is dryness and distance and it is difficult to continue. When listening and silence grow in prayer, we are likely to experience moments of intimacy and delight. As we travel through life we discover that the ways we once prayed simply don't work anymore. There are times we feel the fire of love and times when all seems like ashes. In the course of our prayer lives, a host of different stances/modes/dispositions of the Holy Presence, the Great Mystery, await us.

As we make this journey in and with God's spirit, we taste what we call becoming a saint—being one with the Spirit and all of creation. In the twenty-first century, we don't look for saints who sit on a pole like Simon Stylites, starve themselves or live in a cave in the desert. We look for "saints" who are present to the world of the twenty-first century and who respond to its needs with integrity and character. We want our "saints" to live the social dimensions of the faith as global citizens.[8] We long to see reflected in one another a commitment to four qualities of a spiritual way of being in the world discovered centuries ago as each of the world religions emerged. Though the leaders of these religions had no contact with one another, common marks of the spiritual way arose. Those are: the golden rule—Do unto others as you would have them do to you; a recognition of the spark of the Divine in every human being; the centrality of compassion; and a commitment to nonviolence. These marks are as relevant in the twenty-first century as they were in 9 BC.[9]

No one has arrived. That is why the journey itself is home. Believe that being a twenty-first–century saint is possible, and, in fact, your calling. I heard a woman say that she saw something of God each hour of the twenty-four. That is "home." Another woman faithfully offered her life to God in a single prayer each morning and each evening. That is "home." I met a woman who sees and feels the interconnectedness of all things. That is "home." I know a couple who lost their first longed-for baby—born early and with health problems. They held him, baptized him, buried him and still believe in loving Mystery. That is "home."

God is making all things new. We can be part of that creative process. We can be midwives of a new creation by opening ourselves to life and to amazing grace. A vibration travels through the universe when it senses the liberating presence of a traveler who has embraced the way of transformation. That vibration is the wonder of cocreation and coredemption. We are all meant to be a part of it—all of us in any walk of life, any age, any class, any race. A translation of Paul's letter to the Romans expresses well the vitality of this journey: "The whole creation is on tiptoe to see the wonderful sight of the sons and daughters of God coming into their own" (Romans 8:19).[10]

Coming into their own is coming home. And the transforming journey is home. It is available to us every day of our lives right in the place where we live.

FOOD FOR THOUGHT

1. In one sense, we are always on a threshold about to be transformed—to cross over to a renewed way of being. At the side of a bed where birth, surgery or death are imminent, the one keeping vigil and the one in the bed are on a threshold. What threshold in your life does this sentence bring to mind? What were your feelings? How did you pray? How did that threshold and your response affect your life in the long-term?

2. The transformational journey is all about loving God, neighbor and self in free and unfettered ways. In the past year of your life, how have you let go of something or lived through some experience that freed you to love in a better way?

3. How does allowing the sorrow of the world to invade your consciousness change you? When your mind and heart are touched by Darfur, global war victims, women harmed and hurt, how do you express yourself in prayer?

RITUAL

1. Gather a candle and a globe (or a picture or symbol of the Earth). After taking some time to breathe slowly and deeply, read and ponder this poem:

> You, God, who live next door—
>
> If at times, through the long night, I trouble you

with my urgent knocking —
this is why: I hear you breathe so seldom.
I know you're all alone in that room.
If you should be thirsty, there's no one
to get you a glass of water.
I wait listening, always. Just give me a sign!
I'm right here.
As it happens, the wall between us
is very thin. Why couldn't a cry
from one of us
break it down? It would crumble
easily,
it would barely make a sound.[11]
(I, 6)

2. Spend some time noticing what lines in the poem have meaning for you. After that, pray the following prayer: My God, I want you to come here, please. I am ready to break the thin wall between us and invite you to share time, life, moments of darkness and light. Show me how to cross a threshold in my life and see how you are present there. Come, Holy Presence, open my heart to the Spirit's gifts and fruits. I want to see your face in all faces.

3. Take some time to be in silence and repeat this line: Be still and know that I am God.

4. Pray in silence for change in the world's people, one heart at a time. If you are with a group, tell a story of some place you have visited on the globe, near or far away, that has made a difference in who you have become. Share what has transformed you, freed you, brought you closer to God. Close your prayer with an embrace of peace and a blessing of the globe.

As women awaken to prayer, may we taste and touch what is eternal and sacred in all of life. That will give us the joy and hope for which the world longs.

Tasting and touching are beautifully sensuous experiences essential to a full human life. And a full human life is naturally spiritual. God's presence permeates everyone and everything in the universe—no exceptions. Grasping this pervasiveness of God makes it clear that there is something lasting and sacred in all we taste and touch. If we are awake to this truth, whether we are thirsting, struggling, nurturing, transforming, tasting or touching, our hands and hearts and prayers are in God. Actually at every moment in every day, we are inhaling and exhaling Divine Life. We don't always notice it, so we need to pray in order to be aware, to open ourselves to transforming love. Any kind of prayer will do that makes us more conscious of Holy Presence and of the Life of God always there and available in ordinary life. "God is waiting for us in everything we touch or that touches us. Everything in the whole world is swimming in a sea of God."[1] The life of Holy Presence and our lives are intimately interwoven; dwelling in that awareness and in some way expressing it is your prayer of all prayer. Every time it dawns on us that we are thus related is time for a song of joy. A sixteenth-century poet-saint of India offers another cause for joy: We can help God comfort the world.

God has
a special
interest in women
for they can lift this world to their breast
and help Him
comfort.[2]

CHAPTER ONE

1. Dorothee Soelle, *The Silent Cry: Mysticism and Resistance* (Minneapolis: Augsburg Fortress, 2001), p. 89.

2. Joan Chittister, *In the Heart of the Temple: My Spiritual Vision for Today's World* (Erie, Pa.: Benetvision, 2004), p. 42.

3. Walter Burghardt, "Contemplation: A Long Loving Look at the Real," *Church*, Winter 1989, p. 15.

4. Rosemary Radford Reuther, *Sexism and God-Talk: Toward a Feminist Theology.* (Boston: Beacon, 1983), p. 80.

5. Cited in Mary Collins, *Women at Prayer* (Madeleva Lecture, 1987) (New York: Paulist, 1987), p. 24.

6. Ann Hillman, *The Dancing Animal Woman: A Celebration of Life* (Norfolk, Conn.: Bramble, 1994), p. 70.

7. Anne Sexton, *The Complete Poems: Anne Sexton* (Boston: Houghton Mifflin, 1981), p. 462.

8. Barbara G. Walker, *The Crone: Woman of Age, Wisdom, and Power* (San Francisco: Harper, 1985), pp. 43–49.

9. Charlene Spretnak, *The Resurgence of the Real: Body, Nature, and Place in a Hypermodern World* (New York: Routledge, 1999), p. 183.

10. Elizabeth A. Johnson, (Madeleva Lecture, 1993), *Women, Earth, and Creator Spirit* (New York.: Paulist, 1993), p. 63.

CHAPTER TWO

1. Mary C. Grey, *Sacred Longings: The Ecological Spirit and Global Culture* (Minneapolis: Augsburg Fortress, 2004), p. 211.

2. Ruth Burrows, O.C.D., *Essence of Prayer* (London: Burns and Oates, 2006), p. 1.

3. Mattie J.T. Stepanek, *Hope Through Heartsongs* (New York: Hyperion, 2002), p. 49.

4. The full title of Garrels's book is *Naked in Baghdad: The Iraq War and the Aftermath as Seen by NPR Correspondent Anne Garrels,* Vint Lawrence, coauthor (New York: Farrar, Straus and Giroux, 2004), p. 131.

5. Cited in Elizabeth A. Johnson, *Women, Earth, and Creator Spirit,* p. 48.

6. Soelle, pp. 20–21.

7. Raimon Panikkar, *The Experience of God: Icons of the Mystery,* Joseph Cunneen, trans. (Minneapolis: Augsburg Fortress, 2006), p. 134.

8. Soelle, p. 20.

9. Cited in Grey, p. 164.

CHAPTER THREE

1. Elizabeth A. Dreyer, *Holy Power, Holy Presence: Rediscovering Medieval Metaphors for the Holy Spirit* (New York: Paulist, 2007), p. 231.

2. Cited in Monica Furlong, ed., *Women Pray: Voices through the Ages, from Many Faiths, Cultures, and Traditions* (Woodstock, Vt.: Skylight Paths, 2001), p. 51.

3. Cited in Grey, p. 121.

4. Cited in Judy Cannato, *Radical Amazement: Contemplative Lessons from Black Holes, Supernovas, and Other Wonders of the Universe* (Notre Dame, Ind.: Sorin, 2006), p. 15.

5. Paul Winter, *Missa Gaia*.

6. Panikkar, p. 19.

7. "Ten Challenges of a Liberated Woman," *What Is Enlightenment?*, July–September, 2007, p. 81.

8. Grey, p. 134.

9. Panikkar, p. 42.

10. Elizabeth A. Johnson, *She Who Is* (New York: Herder, 1999), p. 228.

11. Johnson, *Women, Earth, and Creator Spirit*, p. 91.

CHAPTER FOUR

1. Johnson, , *She Who Is*, pp. 260–261.

2. Anne Sexton, "The Rowing Endeth," *The Complete Poems*, p. 473.

3. Gerald G. May, M.D., *The Dark Night of the Soul: A Pyschiatrist Explores the Connection Between Darkness and Spiritual Growth.* (San Francisco: Harper, 2004), p. 9.

4. Angeles Arrien, *The Second Half of Life: Opening the Eight Gates of Wisdom* (Boulder, Co.: Sounds True, 2005), p. 4.

5. Constance Fitzgerald, "Impasse and Dark Night" in Joann Wolski Conn, ed., *Women's Spirituality: Resources for Christian Development* (New York: Paulist, 1996), p. 415.

6. Alan D. Wolfelt, PH.D., "Companioning vs. Treating: Beyond the Medical Model of Bereavement Caregiving." This keynote address was given at the Association of Death Education and Counseling in Chicago, May, 2003, p. 3.

7. Kristine M. Rankka, *Women and the Value of Suffering: An Aw(e)ful Rowing Toward God* (Collegeville, Minn.: Liturgical, 1998), p. 8.

8. Rankka, p. 224.

9. Daniel Ladinsky, trans., *Love Poems from God: Twelve Sacred Voices from the East and West* (New York: Penguin Compass, 2002), pp. 290–291.

10. Dianne L. Oliver, ed. and intro., *Dorothee Soelle: Essential Writings* (Maryknoll, N.Y.: Orbis, 2006), p. 123.

11. Cited in Grey, pp. 82–83.

12. Grey, p. 169–170.

CHAPTER FIVE

1. Dreyer, p. 236.

2. John Baker Miller, "The Development of Women's Sense of Self," in *Women's Spirituality*, Joann Wolski Conn, ed. (New York: Paulist, 1996), pp. 167–178.

3. I use the Jerusalem Bible translation with one word change here because it expresses best the emphasis I want to make in using the text and it does not change the meaning.

4. Cited in Dreyer, p. 199.

5. Ranya Idliby, Suzanne Oliver and Priscilla Warner, *The Faith Club: A Muslim, A Christian, A Jew—Three Women Search for Understanding* (New York: Free Press, 2006), p. 292.

6. Cannato, p. 70.

7. Hafiz, "The Sun Never Says," from *The Gift*, Daniel Ladinsky, trans. (New York: Penguin, 1999), p. 34.

8. Johnson, *Women, Earth, and Creator Spirit*, p. 67.

9. Cannato, *Radical Amazement*, p. 62.

10. Thich Nhat Hanh, *The Long Road Turns to Joy: A Guide to Walking Meditation* (Berkeley, Calif.: Parallax, 1996), p. 4.

11. Hanh, p. 67.

CHAPTER SIX

1. Cannato, p. 137.

2. Quoted in Jan L. Richardson, *Sacred Journeys: A Woman's Book of Daily Prayer* (Nashville, Tenn.: Upper Room, 1995), p. 102.

3. Kathleen Fischer, *The Courage the Heart Desires: Spiritual Strength in Difficult Times* (San Francisco: Jossey-Bass, 2006), pp. 129–130.

4. Entire text available at Nobelprize.org/peace/laureate/2004.

5. Furlong, p. 166.

6. May, p. 4.

7. May, p. 4.

8. Drew Christiansen, s.j., "Holy Men and Women," *America*. October 29, 2007, p. 12.

9. Karen Armstrong, *The Great Transformation* (New York: Knopf, 2006). This entire book on the Axial Age is about the characteristics of religious traditions held in common.

10. This is a free translation of Romans 8:19. The *NRSV* uses the following words: "For the creation waits with eager longing for the revealing of the children of God."

11. Rainer Maria Rilke, *Rilke's Book of Hours: Love Poems to God*, Anita Barrows and Joanna Macy, trans. (New York: Riverhead, 1996), p. 52.

Epilogue

1. Louis M. Savary, *The Divine Milieu Explained: A Spirituality for the 21st Century* (New York: Paulist, 2007), p. 11.

2. Ladinsky, p. 246.

ADDITIONAL RESOURCES

BOOKS

Bergant, Dianne, Susan Calef and Gregory Polan. *Prayer in the Catholic Tradition.* Liguori, Mo.: Ligouri, 2007.

Broz, Mary Ruth, RSM, Barbara Flynn and Jean Clough. *Midwives of an Unnamed Future: Spirituality for Women in Times of Unprecedented Change.* Skokie, Ill.: ACTA, 2006.

Cannato, Judy. *Radical Amazement: Contemplative Lessons from Black Holes, Supernovas, and Other Wonders of the Universe.* Notre Dame, Ind.: Sorin, 2006.

Collins, Mary. *Women at Prayer* (Madeleva Lecture, 1987). New York: Paulist Press, 1987.

D'Arcy, Paula. *Gift of the Red Bird: The Story of a Divine Encounter.* New York: Crossroad, 2002.

Dreyer, Elizabeth A. *Holy Power, Holy Presence: Rediscovering Medieval Metaphors for the Holy Spirit.* New York: Paulist, 2007.

Fischer, Kathleen. *The Courage the Heart Desires: Spiritual Strength in Difficult Times.* San Francisco: Jossey-Bass, 2006.

Furlong, Monica, ed. and intro. *Women Pray: Voices Through the Ages, from Many Faiths, Cultures, and Traditions.* Woodstock, Vt.: Skylight Paths, 2001.

Gallagher, Blanche. *Meditations with Teilhard de Chardin.* Santa Fe, N.M.: Bear, 1988.

Hanh, Thich Nhat. *The Long Road Turns to Joy: A Guide to Walking Meditation.* Berkeley, Calif.: Parallax, 1996.

Hillesum, Etty. *An Interrupted Life: The Diaries, 1941–1943 and Letters from Westerbork.* New York: Holt, 1996.

Leng, Felicity. *Invincible Spirits: A Thousand Years of Women's Spiritual Writings.* Grand Rapids: Eerdmans, 2007.

May, Gerald G., M.D., *The Dark Night of the Soul: A Pyschiatrist Explores the Connection Between Darkness and Spiritual Growth.* San Francisco: HarperOne, 2004.

Merrill, Nan C. *Psalms for Praying: An Invitation to Wholeness.* New York: Continuum, 2006. This collection of reflections on the psalms introduces a great variety of names for Sacred Presence.

Mortenson, Greg, and David Oliver Relin. *Three Cups of Tea: One Man's Mission to Promote Peace...One School at a Time.* New York: Penguin, 2007.

Reagan, Michael, ed. *The Hand of God: Thoughts and Images Reflecting the Spirit of the Universe.* West Conshohocken, Pa.: Templeton Foundation, 2001.

Rilke, Rainer Maria. *Rilke's Book of Hours: Love Poems to God*, Anita Barrows and Joanna Marie Macy, trans. New York: Riverhead, 2005.

Roth, Nancy. *The Breath of God: An Approach to Prayer.* Cambridge, Mass.: Cowley, 1990.

Silf, Margaret. *The Gift of Prayer: Embracing the Sacred in the Everyday.* New York: Bluebridge, 2005.

Stepanek, Mattie J.T. and Gary Zukav. *Hope Through Heartsongs.* New York: Hyperion, 2002.

Wallace, Mark I. *Finding God in the Singing River.* Minneapolis: Augsburg Fortress, 2005.

OTHER MEDIA

Crash. Lions Gate Films, 2005. Useful for its insights into human nature and change.

Winged Migration. Sony Pictures, 2005.

Brown, Monica. *Quiet My Soul: Mantras and Meditative Songs*, CD. Livermore, Calif.: Emmaus, 2003.

Called to Holiness, CD. Available at www.CalledtoHoliness.org.

WEB RESOURCES

http://www.pray-as-you-go.org/

www.CalledtoHoliness.org. Please take a look at the official Web site for this series for new articles, authors' speaking engagements and other features.

INDEX

Abba experience, 80
Arrien, Angeles, 45
awakening. *See* spiritual awakening

balance, need for, 60–61
baptism, Jesus', 80–81
beauty
    awakening to, 12–13
    saving grace of, 20–21
beholding, as key connection between
    noticing and prayer, 2
Bible, sources for God imagery in, 34
birth, witnessing, as call to conscious-
    ness, 14–15
bodies, women's
    negative notions about, 9
    as sacred vessels, 3–4

Catherine of Siena, 60
change, as constant, 72
Chittister, Joan, 2
community, and women's spirituality,
    21–22
connections, non-hierarchical, 63
contemplation, 61–63
    See also meditation
cosmogenesis, 67
courage
    among women in Stations of the
      Cross, 51–52
    personal acts of, 70
Craighead, Meinrad, 4
creation, desire to be part of, 73–74
critical thinking, and faith, 8
The Crone, 7

dark night of soul, 84–85
Deity, Mother in, 34
Divine
    female dimension of, 34–36

noting qualities of, 39
and relationship to prayer, 1
doubt, being open to considering, 7–8
Dreyer, Elizabeth, 36

evil, doing, against desires, 78–79
evolutionary perspective, 29–30

faith, convictions and doubts about, 9
The Faith Club, 64
family, and women's spirituality, 21–22
friendship
    among women, 63–65
    and women's spirituality, 21–22

Garrels, Anne, 16–17
gender-specific God language, 27
global concerns, and prayer, 88
God
    as "companion-sufferer," 49
    finding heartbeat of, in all
      experience, 19–20
    incomprehensible mystery of,
      28–29, 36
    male images of, 32–33
    names for, 33–37, 56–57
    prayer to get closer to, 88–89
    spiritually mature relationship with,
      27
    transformative work of, 72–73,
      85–87
    unfathomable nature of, 27
    ways of seeing, 37–39
    See also Divine, Jesus
good, wanting but not doing, 78–79
Gospel stories, depicting Jesus as con-
    sistently awake, 13–15
grace, transforming, 75–76
Green Belt movement, 76–77
Grey, Mary, 30
grief, 47–48

Called to Holiness Series

A groundbreaking eight-volume series on women's spirituality, *Called to Holiness: Spirituality for Catholic Women* will cover the many diverse facets of a woman's interior life and help her discover how God works with her and through her. An ideal resource for a woman seeking to find how God charges the moments of her life—from spirituality itself, to the spirituality of social justice, the spirituality of grieving the loss of a loved one, the creation and nurturing of families, the mentoring of young adult Catholic women, to recognition of the shared wisdom of women in the middle years—this series can be used by individuals or in groups. Far from the cloister or monastery, these books find God in the midst of a woman's everyday life and help her to find and celebrate God's presence day to day and acknowledge her own gifts as an ordinary "theologian." The books can be used independently or together for individual discussion or group faith sharing. Each book will include gathering rituals, reflection questions and annotated bibliographies.

Making Sense of God
A Woman's Perspective

Elizabeth A. Dreyer

The moment is ripe for ordinary Catholic women to "do Christian theology." Times such as these challenge us to be holy, to be alive in the Spirit, to summon the energy and make the commitment to help one another grow spiritually. Now is the time for Catholic women to make sense of God.

In this introductory volume to the **Called to Holiness** series, Catholic theologian Elizabeth Dreyer encourages us to acknowledge our dignity, harvest our gifts and empower all women in church and society. Dreyer helps us to shape what we think about God, justice, love, prayer, family life, the destiny of humanity and the entire universe.

Release: August 2008
Religion — Spirituality
Paper, 128 pp.
Order #B16884
ISBN 978-0-86716-884-6
$11.95

Called to Holiness Series

Called to Holiness Publication Schedule

Fall 2008:

• Making Sense of God:
A Woman's Perspective
(Elizabeth A. Dreyer)
ISBN 978-0-86716-884-6

• Grieving With Grace:
A Woman's Perspective
(Dolores R. Leckey)
ISBN 978-0-86716-888-4

• Living a Spirituality of
Action: A Woman's
Perspective (Joan Mueller)
ISBN 978-0-86716-885-3

Spring 2009:

• Embracing Latina
Spirituality: A Woman's
Perspective
(Michelle A. Gonzalez)
ISBN 978-0-86716-886-0

• Awakening to Prayer:
A Woman's Perspective
(Clare Wagner)
ISBN 978-0-86716-892-1

Fall 2009:

• Creating New Life,
Nurturing Families:
A Woman's Perspective
(Sidney Callahan)
ISBN 978-0-86716-893-8

• Weaving Faith and
Experience: A Woman's
Perspective on the Middle
Years (Patricia Cooney
Hathaway)
ISBN 978-0-86716-904-1

• Finding My Voice:
A Young Adult Woman's
Perspective
(Beth M. Knobbe)
ISBN 978-0-86716-894-5

Called to Holiness Companion CD
Musical selections to accompany the gathering rituals for the book series. Order #A9001 **$19.95**

Grieving With Grace
A Woman's Perspective

Dolores R. Leckey

There are many ways in which the course of our daily lives can be altered—illness, change in residence, loss of employment and death of loved ones. These alterations can require dramatic and even subtle changes in our everyday living, limit our options and force us to choose different priorities.

Dolores Leckey knows firsthand that the death of a spouse changes forever the rhythms of life at all levels—body, mind and soul. In this moving and personal narrative that includes entries from her journal, she shares with us her own shift in consciousness, in the way she sees God, herself and the world after her husband's death. She offers us consolation and hope.

Release: August 2008
Religion — Spirituality
Paper, 112 pp.
Order #B16888
ISBN 978-0-86716-888-4
$11.95